The Glorious Resurrection

By
Professor Hilton Hotema

978-1-63923-440-0

Printed: October 2022

Cover Art By: Amit Paul

Published and Distributed By:
Lushena Books
607 Country Club Drive, Unit E
Bensenville, IL 60106
www.lushenabks.com

ISBN: 978-1-63923-440-0

THE GLORIOUS RESURRECTION

Prologue

PERFECTION

The Blazing Star of Bethlehem
Is actually the Godly Man
The God I put up in the sky
Is just another phase of I
I am He to whom I prayed
The He to whom I looked for aid
I am He whom I did seek
I am My Own mountain peak
I do upon Creation look
As a part of My Own book
For I'm the One the many make
Of Matter which from Me I take
For all is Me; there are no Two
Creation is Myself all thru.
When I'm born I think I live
And when I die I think I give
My life away, to Live no more.
Then I dream of the Golden Shore,
Which I shall see in the Resurrection
And find at last My Own Perfection.

Glorious Resurrection
By Prof. Hilton Hotema.

P R O L O G U E

Search the Scriptures, for in them ye think ye have Eternal Life (John 5:39), and they are they which testify of the Fable relating to the Crucified and

Resurrected God.

That Fable was not invented to present a fairy tale about a Savior of the World, but to teach a profound lesson of Life. That lesson if the subject of this work.

You greatly fear the Demon of Death; you have heard much about the Future Life; you have read books and heard sermons on these subjects, but you were disappointed by the arguments presented, for the authors cited no law to support their claims.

You realize that we live in a Universe of law and order, you are not convinced as to the factuality of the Future Life unless a definite phase of Universal Law is

cited to satisfy you that (a) the Death of the Body (b) is not the end of Man, nor (c) the extinction of Life, as alleged by science.

And your intelligence will not allow you to accept the unscientific postulate interpolated in the Bible by the Church Fathers, that "God so loved the world (a little insignificant speck in space), that he gave

his only begotten Son, that whosoever believeth in him should not perish but have everlasting life" (John 3:16).

You know that Life is ruled by law, not by what man believes. You are too wise to be influenced by that fraudulent interpolation in the Bible.

It fails to harmonize with the law, and also with the declaration of Paul in the Bible, to the effect that --

"We shall not sleep (in death), but we shall all be changed (by death to im-

mortality),   and the dead shall be raised incorruptible.... For This corruptible

(body) must put on incorruption, and this mortal (body) must put on immortality.....

and (then) Death is swallowed up in victory.

O Death, where is thy sting? O Grave, where is thy victory?"--1 Cor. 15:51, 54,55.

We shall show in this dissertation that this noted Pythagorean Philosopher of the first century, from whose writings most of the New Testament was compiled and

who died some two hundred fifty years before the world ever heard of the Church Jesus, not only was well versed in the Law of Creation, but realized that the expiration of

the Body is not the extinction of Life.

To drive this important message of Light thru the dense wall of darkness in which sixteen hundred years of intensive brain-washing and mind-conditioning has

imprisoned the sheep, it will be imperative for us to peck and pound on Paul's assertion of Transition, to wake up the orthodox reader so he can see, by the dawn of
reason, the Glorious Vision of the Future Life which the Wise Masters concealed in

their famous Fable of the Crucified God and his Resurrection.

The great doctors of the day frankly declare that we have no science of Man; but
the rank and file know not the reason why. The sheep little suspect that such a

science would explode to atom almost all that is taught by the Mother Church and by
Medical Art. So these sordid institutions of darkness happily join hands in the job

of preventing the Light of Knowledge from penetrating the skulls of the hoodwinked
masses.

The logical result of this cunning trick is a treacherous sea of ignorance that
surrounds the Field of Biology, and the gullible masses grope in the fog, seeking the

doctors to relieve the pains in thei bodies, and the preachers to relieve the darkness in their minds.

What is foolishly termed science in the Field of Biology, is a stupid system of
now-outmoded Materialism that developed during the ignorance of the 19th century, in

opposition to the stupid supernaturalism of the Church, which intelligent men could
not swallow.

The postulate of Evolutionism marks a long stride forward in man's thinking, but
it fell into the error of judging by sight the processes of Creation, thus accepting
as Life the function of the Form instead of its being the cause of the function.

According to this theory of science, when the Form ceases to function, that is the
extinction of Man and the termination of Life.

Now follow closely this ancient line of reasoning: The Form is a Created Body,
whereas the Animative Force that vitalizes the Form is an Uncreated Entity.

The Created Form is constantly changing. That is the reason why man must breathe
and drink and eat. But the Uncreated Entity, the existence of which science recog-

nizes by terming it the Unknown, is a mysterious element within the Created Form
which survives all changes in the Form and all changes in the particles of which the
Form is composed.

Natural phenomena is the product of a Creative Force. We constantly witness its
workings and the Law of its operations. Science should be a sensible description of
that Force and a logical interpretation of its governing Law.

But instead of that, science produces confusion in which its leaders are lost,
by denying the existence of that Force at one time, and conceding its existence at
another.

Science admits that there is in the Created Body of Man an Unknown Element that
is not understood, and then attempts lightly to dispose of the puzzle by asserting

that this Unknown Element rises from the function of the Created Body.

That truly great scientist, Dr. Alexis Carrel, asserted that "Man is made up of a procession of phantoms, in the midst of which there strides an Unknowable Reality" (Man The Unknown, p.4).

After conceding the existence of the "Unknowable Reality," and admitting its superiority by placing it above "phantoms," Carrel then made no definite attempt to

analyze its nature. Instead, he frankly confessed that, "For the present, it is impossible to grasp the constitution of the human body" (p. 109).

And so, upon the testimony of one of the greatest scientists of this century, we are told that we have no Science of Man, no Science of Anthropology, no Science of Biology, no Science of Psychology, no Science of Physiology, and no Science of Pathology.

How could it be worse? We can't go any lower. We are now on the bottom. And the controlled press is filled with items about

"the March of Science."

The only Science of Man which the world has ever had, was that developed by the Atlantean Astrologers over a period of fifty thousand years or more, and then frantically destroyed in the 4th, 5th, and 6th centuries by the Mother Church in order to

conceal the astrological nature of its spurious religious system.

Some fragments of that science have slipped into the Bible, and by piecing them together like a jig-saw-puzzle, we are able to salvage the essence of that ancient

science and thus to interpret most of the symbols and allegories in which it was concealed.

We observe that Two Bodies are definitely mentioned in the Bible, and they were analyzed by the great philosopher Paul.

Science has never considered it important to pay any particular attention to these Two Bodies, and regards Paul's statements as just more

"heathenish superstition." And yet, a scientific determination of these Two Bodies would dispel most all of the mystery that makes Man and Life such an enigma to us.

In discussing these Two Bodies, Paul said that one is Terrestraial and the other is Celestial; the one is Natural and the other is Spiritual

(Astral); the one is Corruptible, the other is Incorruptible; the one is Mortal, the other Immortal (1 Cor.15th chap.).

The entire mystery of Man and Life is involved and concealed in these statements of Paul. Right here we have the pivotal doctrine of our work.

And consistency of thought demands that we proceed in our course in a direct manner, thru infinite time to infinite results.

The Clergy make a blundering attempt to differentiate between these Two Bodies. They are incompetent to do more. And science sneeringly terms the statements of Paul the vaporings of "superstitious heathens."

Now for a highly important point: We must notice that the Creative Cycle of the Universe shows to him who can think, that Created Bodies have beginnings and must have endings. This fact applies without exception to all Created Bodies. The Earth, the Sun, the Stars, all these are Created Bodies. They had a beginning and must have and ending.

But, according to the Bible, the Uncreated Entity that animates the Created Human Body, and is the direct and definite cause of all its functions, had no beginning, and, consequently, will never have and ending. It is as eternal and everlasting as the very elements of which the Earth and the Sun are made.

This is powerful philosophy for the weak minds of this civilization, and for the distorted and unbalanced minds of the Preachers and the Doctors. And yet that scientific datum was known to and recognized by those "superstitious heathens" of the Ancient World. It was recorded by them in their scrolls, and, perhaps by chance some of it slipped into the Bible, especially in Proverbs, where it is written:

"I (Uncreated Entity) was set up (existed) from everlasting, ... or ever the earth was.... Before the mountains were settled, before the hills, was I (Uncreated Entity) brought forth.... When he (Creative Principle) prepared the heavens, (Uncreated Entity) was there" (Prov. 8:22-27).

There it is, right in the Bible. Now will you believe it?

And we shall further show in this discussion, and cite the law to support our statements, that the Ancient Astrologers had their feet on solid ground and knew whereof they spoke, when they declared:

"O Death, I will be thy plague. O Grave, I will be thy destruction (Ho.13:14). Death is swallowed up in victory (Isa.25:8). I (Uncreated Entity) am he that liveth and was dead (while inhabiting the Created Body); and behold, I am alive for evermore (Rev.1:18). And there shall be no more death, neither sorrow, nor cying, neither shall there be any more pain; for the former things (Created Bodies) are passed away (Rev. 21:4).

One wise doctor understood this ancient philosophy, and he wrote: "There is no Birth without Death, and no Death without a Resurrection.

All action in the entire Universe is absolutely dependent for its continuity upon Cyclic Change; and as surely as Day follows Night, so must Life follow Death"(Dr. James Clark, In Eternal Time).

It is only thru the Cyclic Change called Death that the Uncreated Entity is liberated from confinement in the Created Body, and thus passes on to the Future Life

in the Glorious Astral World.

That was also the Born Again Doctrine of the Ancient Astrologers, and the subject of their famous Fable of the Crucified and Resurrected God. That Fable, as we

shall see, covered and concealed the Ancient Doctrine of the Future Life.

In connection with this work, the student is urged to read the Folios by Prof. Hotema as follows:

1. Cosmic Creation (2nd ed.)   3. The Flame Divine
2. Pre-Existence Of Man   4. The Soul's Secret.

Manila, P. I., 1960 A.D.   Prof. Hilton Hotema, in his 83rd year.

CHAPTER I

S Y M B O L I S M

The notion that there is a higher knowledge which surpasses all common knowledge and is inaccessible to the unprepared mind, permeates the entire history of human thought. According to certain memorials of past ages, a profound knowledge, quite different from that taught in the schools, formed the essence of the philosophy of the Sacred Wisdom of the Ancient Masters.

The task of discovering traces of this ancient knowledge is the work of the archeologist, who excavates for the evidence of ancient civilizations and finds that evidence buried beneath several strata of ruins left by those who lived and vanished thousands of years ago.

In his work titled Cosmic Creation, 2nd edition, Prof. Hotema describes the ruins of cities so old that they were built before there were any mountains on the earth. The Bible mentions a time before the mountains were brought forth (Ps.90:2).

One of these cities was found in South America, on the very roof of the world, upon the now barren, bleak and dreary plateau that exists between the two ranges of the Andes. Irrefutable evidences are present to show that when the city was built, perhaps millions of years ago, the land on which it stands was just above sealevel, nearly three miles below the present site.

Such discoveries yield valuable evidence in the form of symbols carved on stone temples and monuments, which contain and yet conceal the factual essence of this ancient knowledge.

Only a symbol can deliver us from the slavery of misleading words and formulas, and enable us to attain to the higher level of thinking freely. Scholastics bring to the ultimate analysis only words, and these are entirely artificial, while their meaning is often deceptive.

By its very nature, a word is an instrument of paradox. Any theme can be presented and defended by the means of argumentation. This is so because every discipline deals not with realities that reach our consciousness by themselves, but only their oral representations which meet the fantasies of our mind, and our mind is often unreliable and frequently allows itself to be deceived with this false coin of our thoughts.

The Sacred Wisdom of the Ancient Masters is distinguished by its being able to move away from words and to immerse itself in the contemplation of the elements taken by themselves in their own true essence.

And furthermore, the philosophy of the Ancient Masters, which dealt with the nature of Life and the constitution of Man, was always more or less occult, in the sense that it was cloaked in fable and fiction and passed on its teachings under the cover of enigmas, allegories and symbols, the true meanings of which have baffled the best intellect of the modern world, leading to the logical conclusion that they were the work of "superstitious heathens" who had little else to do, and spent much of their time in carving apparently meaningless designs.

Then there came a surprising discovery that opened the book of the forgotten past in the shape of the famous Rosette Stone, a picture of which appears in Prof. Hotema's work titled the Land of Light.

This remarkable Stone was found by chance, buried in the delta of the Nile, where it had without doubt been buried by the Faithful Church Fathers, with the expectation that it would never be found. It required years of study to interpret the inscription on the Stone, which proved to be lengthy proclamation in hieroglyphics that was paralleled in Greek.

Eureka! At last was found the Key so seriously needed by the researchers to enable them to piece together life a jig-saw-puzzle, some four thousand years of Egyptian history, and reveal the secret meaning of the ancient symbols which must have originated in the magnificent Mother land of Mu, sometimes called Lemuiria, and from there found their way to various lands of the ancient world.

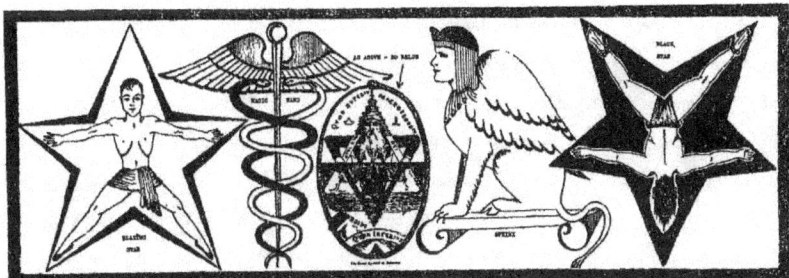

person; and yet the correct interpretation of these strange designs reveals surprising secrets as to the nature of Life and the constitution of Man which are still unknown to modern science. In fact, this amazing knowledge uncovers the very heart of the Sacred Wisdeom. A detailed interpretation of these symbols appears in the work of Prof. Hotema titled the Sacred Wisdom of the Ancients (Living Fire).

Due to the loss and destruction of the Ancient Scrolls, leading scholars were unable to interpret the meaning of the five symbols shown above until the early part of the 19th century. Even now only a few leading occultists have been able to interpret these symbols in agreement with the Sacred Wisdom of the Ancients.

1. The chief symbol in the center is the Interlaced Triangles. This design represents the dual bodies of Man, discussed in detail in this work. The lower body is termed in the Bible "our earthly house," and the upper body, the "house not made with hands, eternal in the heavens" (2 Cor.5:1).

2. The Black Pentacle with Man standing on his head, represents the black or lower portion of the Interlaced Triangles, and presents what the Ancient Masters taught as the Birth of Man in the physical world. In their philosophy, this was the Death of the Astral God, and was called the Crucifixion.

3. The Blazing Star with Man standing upright on his feet and head up in "the clouds," represents the white or upper portion of the Interlaced Triangles, and presents what the Ancient Masters taught as the Death of Man in the physical world. In their philosophy, this was the Birth of the Astral God, the Born Again Doctrine of

the Bible (John 3:3,5,7), and was called the Resurrection.

This was the Unknown Joy Of Death which was elucidated to the Neophyte upon initiation in the Ancient Mysteries, and he then understood the meaning of the statement, "Better is the Day of thy Death than the Day of thy Birth" (Eccl. 7:1).

4. The Sphinx, the image of which is found in ancient lands in all parts of the world, represents the Sacred Four Elements of which the earth and every thing upon it are constituted, termed by the Ancient Masters Fire, Air, Water, Earth, and which correspond in their meaning to the four letters J H V H, which the Church Fathers arbitrarily vowelized to produce the word JeHoVaH, and the Church God adopted it as a new name for himself (Ex.6:3).

In the Bible the Sphinx is mentioned as Four Beasts, full of eyes before and behind, before the throne. "The first beast was like a lion, and the second beast like a calf, and the third beast had a face as a man, and the fourth beast was like a flying eagle" (Rev.4:67).

5. The Magic Wand (Caduceus) symbolizes the Creative Principle, called the Double Law by the Ancient Masters. The upright Staff represents the Spinal Column, and the Globe at the top represents man's head. The Wings represent Air and also Mind; the two Serpents represent the positive and negative aspects of the polar force which flow up and down the Spinal Cord, a detailed description of which appears in Prof. Hotema's work titled the Son Of Perfection, the reading of which will shock the student, as it reveals secret knowledge of the Ancient Masters as to the nature of Life and the Constitution of Man unknown to modern science.

The Law of Polarity explains the universal division of all elements, forces and objects into pairs of opposites, called positive and negative, active and inert, initiative and passive, male and female.

The Dual Aspects of Polarity are frequently mentioned in the Bible, but in terms understood only by leading occultists. They are referred to as two olive trees in the 4th chapter of Zechriah, and also as the two Golden Pipes which empty the Golden Oil out of themselves.

One of the great secrets of physiology, unknown to modern science, is concealed in this fable.

- 9-

These are the two anointed ones, the two witnesses, the two aspects of Polar Force, "that stand by the lord of the whole earth" (Zech.4:14).

This "Lord of the whole earth" is Man, and the way in which the two aspects of Polar Force "stand by the Lord" will amaze the student when he reads the interpretation of it in Son Of Perfection.

The surprising feature appears in the fact that the Ancient Masters knew so much about the nature of Life and the Constitution Of Man which modern science has not yet discovered.

CHAPTER II

Ancient Science

We have been assured in good faith by the Mother Church, that the ancient pagans who produced the scrolls from which the Christian Bible was compiled, were nothing but a group of "superstitious heathens." It seems highly inconsistent to put so much faith and trust in the Bible as the Christians do, while considering so dumb and unreliable the authors of the scrolls.

However, the Church endeavors to improve the picture by declaring that among these heathenish pagans there were some "Godly Inspired Men." It is a mighty big jump from such a deep ditch up to such a high level, but we must believe it because the Church teaches it.

The Christian World has no Science of Man, according to the great scientist, Dr. Alexis Carrel, and that constrained him to title his remarkable book, Man the Unknown.

The Ancient Masters developed a Science of Man that is so far ahead of our knowledge and understanding, that we are unable to comprehend the meaning of much of their terminology.

Some occult students in the field of Anthropology and Biology have shown that

-10-

the last book of the Bible is devoted exclusively to the human body and its processes. It describes in fable and fiction certain functions of certain glands that are so far over the head of modern anatomists and physiologists, that the best scholars who have tried to interpret this biblical fable and fiction, assert that the book of Revelation treats of mundane conditions which are, and mundane conditions that shall be.

For centuries attempts were made by the religionists to give the Apoclayse an historical interpretation. Failing in this, it was next interpreted as prophecy. Then Emanuel Swedenborg moved in with his mystic skill, and wrote a book of 1200 pages in which he did his best to explain the Apocalypse.

He explained nothing. He increased the confusion. He walked in the path of his precedessors by viewing the book in the Christian light. Like those before him, he believed the book treated of "heaven and the church." The Master who compiled it from a very ancient Hindu scroll that was written thousands of years before the world ever heard of the gospel Jesus, knew about synagogs, but never heard the word "church, and knew that "heaven" is not a place in space, but a state of the Mind, and said so (Rom.14:17).

In 1953 Prof. Hotema compiled an interpretation of Revelation, which was published by Health Research in 1956 under the title, "Son of Perfection," and showed that Revelation deals not with "heaven and the church," but with the human body and certain of its functions which are still unknown to modern science.

The philosophy of the Ancient Masters did not relate to the worship of an imaginary God far off in space as Christianity teaches and believes. It was a scientific system of Psycho-Bio-Physiology, based upon universal forces and cosmic elements, scientifically designated in their great symbol, the Zodiakos, which indicated the effect of these forces and elements upon Man, the God of the earth (Gen.1:28).

This Astrological Science, hated and condemned by the Mother church, explains in symbol and allegory the ruling effect of the Constellations of the Zodiac upon everything on the earth, including Man. Science has conceded at last that the Moon does have a definite effect upon the earth and its inhabitants; and yet that tiny spec in space is the most insignificant of all the astral bodies known to us. Some of the giant stars are thousands of times larger than our Sun.

Because of the marked deficiency in our knowledge of the nature of Life and the Constitution of Man, we are amazed as we advance to discover that what we have gratuitously assumed to be the product of primitive naivete and paganish superstition, is now found to be the variegated cloak of a recondite wisdom. Not only do the ancient fables and strange symbols bear the impress of genious competent to portray universal forces in cosmic figures and ludicrous fiction, but these ancient scientists register an equal skill in their artful concealment. The employment by these sages of the crafty disguise has carried them so far beyond us in knowledge and skill, that we have been gulled for centuries into accepting the disguise for the real thing.

For instance, they disguised their great Doctrine of the Future Life in their ingenious fable of a Crucified and Resurrected God; and we of the modern world have been duped for sixteen hundred years into embracing this fable for a factual event in human history.

We have discovered that ancient science taught that every sun and every star has its particular nature, property and function, the seal and character of which is impressed by its radiation upon the mineral, vegetal, animal and humanal kingdoms. Even science now admits this to be a fact. And yet our censored dictionaries and encyclopedias call Astrology "the pseudo science" of the pagans, who "ignorantly supposed that the heavenly bodies had certain effects and influences on mundane affairs and human character."

We have discovered that the Zodiac was actually designed as an epitome of the universal pattern of Cosmic Creation in constant operation, incessantly constructing and destroying, dissolving and resurrecting, integrating and disintegrating everything everywhere in an endless circle. We show poor judgment to call a system pseudodoxial simply because it goes over our head and we are not competent to understand it.

The Zodiacal Symbolism reveals to him who is able to interpret its meaning, the interesting story of the creation of the human body from the central seed to the matured organism, and the return, in due course, of its unknown Animative Entity to the Celestial World of peace and pleasure via the natural process of Death and Resurrection. Proper knowledge of this mysterious event enables us to realize the reason why the Ancient Masters

-12-

taught that the Day of Death is better than the Day of Birth.

The Zodiac is also a symbol of the physical garment which fits the God of the earth for his perilous journey thru the Terrestrial World, and is worn by him during his physical peregrinations. The Zodiac also teaches us that at the moment of his birth upon the terrestrial plane, the body of the God corresponds in color, number and vibration with the Solar System at that particular time.

That scientific data may be "pseudo science" to modern scholars, but it will change for them into a real science of the highest order when they learn more about Creation, Life and Man.

This ancient science, dealing with the relationship existing between the Microcosm and the Macrocosm, the Made and the Maker, the Created and the Creator, was presented for thousand years in dramatic form in the Ancient Mysteries, and used for the edification of the Neophyte, the Man of Darkness who was searching for Light, and who was symbolized in the Temples of the Masters by the Black Pentacle, which indicated incarnation, physical birth, or confinement of the Solar Spark in the human body (1 Cor.3:16).

Initiation had for its purpose the instruction of the God of the earth in the mysteries of his being, of his creation, and of his destiny. When he had passed thru the impressive Ritual of Initiation in the Ancient Mysteries, he then became the real God of the earth. He was raised up by what he was taught from the common level of understanding to a higher plane of Consciousness, was clad in a vesture dyed red as a mark of distinction, and was given a new name. That new name was not The Word of God as falsely stated in the Bible (Rev. 19:13). He was called the Son Of Light, and his symbol then was changed to the Blazing Star of Bethlehem, which signified his passage from the Terrestrial World of corruption and mortalism to the Celestial World of incorruption and immortalism, via the Glorious Resurrection.

Master Masons pass thru this ritualism without realizing what it means, nor can the Master of Ceremonies inform them, because he does not know.

The Bible was compiled from the ancient scrolls, but the story it tells is far different from the story contained in those scrolls. It requires the skill of an expert in occultism to uncover in the Bible the "meat in the Nut", and to sift the precious grain from the worthless chaff. He who can do that, discovers the essence of the Hidden Bible and the Sacred Wisdom of the Ancient Masters.

CHAPTER III

Crucified Saviors

"The World's Sixteen Crucified Saviors." Shocking! Impossible! Unbelievable! The Christian Bible teaches that there was only one.

Kersey Graves wrote a book of 436 pages, published in 1875, in which he related the "History of Sixteen Heathen Crucified Gods," and added these statements:

1. The cardinal religious conceptions of all bibles are essentially the same—all running in parable grooves.

2. Every chapter of every bible is but a transcript of the mental chart of the writer.

3. No bible contains anything surpassing the natural, mental and moral capacity of the writer to originate. And hence no divine aid nor inspiration was necessary for its production.

Graves asserts that '"many of the most important facts collated in this work were derived from Sir Godfred Higgins' Anacelypsis, a work as valuable as it is rare—a work comprising the result of twenty years' labor devoted to the investigation of religious history" (p.11).

The Crucified Saviors listed by Graves are as follows:

1. Crucifixion of thulis of Egypt, 1700 B.C. His history is illustrated in the sculptures, made more than 3600 years ago, of a small, retired chamber lying nearly over the western adytum of the temple. Twenty-eight lotus plants near his grave indicate the number of years he lived on earth. After suffering a violent death, he was buried, but rose again, ascended into heaven, and there became "the judge of the dead.

2. Crucifixion of Chrishna of India, 1200 B.C. Mr. Moore, an English traveler and author, in a large collection of drawings taken from Hindu scriptures and monuments, which he arranged together in a work titled "The Hindu Pantheon," has one representing, suspended on the cross, the

Hindu God and Son of God, "our Lord and Savior" Chrishna, with holes pierced in his feet, intended to represent the nail-holes made in the act of crucifixion. To his collar or shirt there hangs an emblem of a heart, represented in the same manner as those attached to the imaginary likeness of Jesus.

3. Crucifixion of Crite of Chaldea, 1200 B.C. He was called "The Redeemer," and was styled "the ever Blessed Son of God,""the Savior of the Race." And when he was crucified, both heaven and earth were shaken to their foundations.

4. Crucifixion of Atys of Phrygia, 1170 B.C. Several histories are given of him, but all concur in representing him as having been an atoning offering for sin. He was suspended on a tree, crucified, buried, and rose again.

5. Crucifixion of Thammuz of Syria, 1160 B.C. The poet has perpetuated his memory in rhyme:

> "Trust, ye saints, your Lord restored,
> Trust ye in your risen Lord;
> For the pains which Thammuz endured
> Our salvation have procured."

6. Crucifixion of Hesus of the Celtic Druids, 834 B.C. He was crucified with a lamb on one side and an elephant on the other. In this symbolical representation of the crucifixion, the elephant, being the largest world, while the lamb, from its proverbial innocent nature, was chosen to represent the innocency of the crucified god.

7. Crucifixion of Indra of Thibet, 725 B.C. Pictures of this god show he was nailed to a cross; there are five wounds, representing the four nail holes and the piercing of his side, as in the case of the gospel Jesus. He walked upon the water and also upon the air, and could fortell future events with perfect accuracy.

8. Crucifixion of Bali of Orissa, 725 B.C. Bali was also called Baliu and Bel. Monuments of him, bearing great age, are found amidst the ruins of the magnificent city of Mahabalipore, partially buried amongst the figures of the temple.

9. Crucifixion of Iao of Nepaul, 622 B.C. He was crucified on a tree.

10. Crucifixion of Sakia of India, 600 B.C. He was also known as Budha Sakia or Sakia Muni.

11. Crucifixion of Alcestos of Euripides, 600 B.C.

12. Crucifixion of Mithra of Persia, 600 B.C. A marble bas-relief in London shows, in the center, the tauroctonous Mithra with the torch-bearers surrounded by the twelve signs of the Zodiac. In the lower corners busts of the Winds; in the upper corners the Sun on his quadriga, and the Moon on a chariot drawn by bulls. Mithra was reputedly born December 25th and crucified on a tree. His worship continued into the 5th century A.D. before it was finally crushed by the Roman Catholic Church.

13. Crucifixion of Quexalcote of Mexico, 587 B.C. The evidence of his crucifixion is tangible, explicit, unequivocal, ineffaceable, and is indelibly engraven on steel and metal plates.

The "Mexican Antiquities" (vol.6,p.66) says "Quexalcote is represented in the paintings of 'Codex Borgianus' as nailed to the cross." Sometimes two thieves are represented as having been crucified with him.

Many other incidences are found related of him in his sacred biography, in which appears the most striking counterparts to the more modern gospel story of Jesus, such as his forty days' fasting and temptation, his riding on an ass, his purification in the temple, his baptism and regeneration by water, his forgiving of sins, being anointed with oil, etc.

14. Crucifixion of Wittoba of the Telingonese, 552 B.C. Higgins said, "He is represented in his history with nail-holes in his hands and in his feet."

15. Crucifixion of Prometheus, 547 B.C. The modern story of this crucified

god, which represents him as having been bound to a rock for thirty years, while vultures preyed upon his vitals, is "an impious Christian fraud," said Sir Godfred Higgins; and this learned religious historian adds: "For I've seen the account which declares he was nailed to a cross with hammer and nails" (Anac.Vol.1, 327).

16. Crucifixion of Quirinus of Rome, 506 B.C. The story of his crucifixion and resurrection closely resembles that of the biblical Jesus.

17. Crucifixion of the biblical Jesus, about 34 A.D. This Jesus appears very insignificant in connection with most of these other crucified gods. All history ignores him, and Graves said:

"The fact that no history, sacred or profane--that not one of the three hundred histories of that age,--makes the slightest allusion to Christ, nor any of the miraculous incidents ingrafted into his life, certainly proves, with a cogency that no logic can overthrow, no sophistry can contradict, and no honest skepticism can resist, that there was never such a miraculously endowed being as his orthodox disciples claim him to have been" (p.322).

18. Masonry has its murdered and resurrected god also. The Master Mason degree is based upon the ancient Tarot, Cards 3 and 20. The meaning of the whole story of the assassination, the burial, the finding and the raising of this god, called Hiram Abiff, is made plain by considering the story in connection with that of the other slain and resurrected gods.

The "G" of Masonry, found traced upon the breast of the murdered Hiram, is the Hebrew letter Gimel. High twelve, the time the Master was attacked, is represented by the mid-day position of the Sun. Low twelve, the time he was buried, is indicated by the position of the moon at the nadir.

Hiram's grave, which is six feet due east and west, and six feet perpendicular, is represented by the six-sided cube upon which Isis sits in Tarot Card 3. The sprig of acacia marking the grave is presented in the Tarot by a scepter in the left hand of Isis, crowned by the symbol of Venus, indicating the power of generation. The twelve Masons sent out to search for Hiram are symbolized by the twelve stars in the Crown of Isis. The five points of fellowship upon which Hiram was resurrected by means of the Lion's paw grip, are indicated by the five eyes inscribed upon the cube. And the final transcendent result of so being resurrected is pictured by the Eagle on the left hand of Isis, which represents the Ego liberated from its dark prison, the human body.

We must not continue along this line at this point, or we'll reveal the ancient secret involved in the fabulous crucifixion and resurrection of a god. That comes later.

Graves wrote a wonderful book, and he who reads it will quickly grasp the absurdity of the claims of the Church regarding its Jesus. But, like other authors, Graves missed the Universal Principle indicated and yet concealed in the fictitious crucifixion and resurrection of gods. He did not even remotely suspect it had any relation to the Doctrine of the Future Life.

CHAPTER IV

Great Mother of the Gods

Prof. Franz Cumont was born January 3, 1868, and educated at Ghent, Bonn, Berlin and Paris, lived in Brussels, and for years was Professor in the University of Ghent.

He was the author of several important works on religion and the ancient gods. In 1909 he finished one titled "Oriental Religions In Roman Paganism," in which he said:

"The first Oriental religion adopted by the Romans was that of the Goddess of Phrygia," and she "received the name of Magna Mater Deum Idea in the Occident."

The Magna Mater was Cybele, and she was the Great Mother Of The Gods. The history of her worship in Rome, said Cumont, "covers six hundred years," and added:

"We can trace each phase of the transformation that changed it, in the course of time, from a collection of very primitive nature beliefs into a sytem of spiritualized mysteries, used by some as a weapon against Christianity" (after that later system was born).

This system originated as "a collection of very primitive nature beliefs," and in the course of time the scheming priesthood gradually transformed it "into a system of spiritualized mysteries," because the "mysterious" and the "unknown" are factors which attract most strongly the mind-conditioned masses whose thinking is done for them.

In dictionaries and encyclopedias that have not been censored by the agents of the Mother Church, Cybele is listed and described as the Great Mother of the Gods. A long account of her appears in the 13th edition of the Encyclopedia Britannica.

Nearly four thousand years ago, this Oriental-Greek-Roman Goddess was worshipped as the Great Mother Of The Gods. And in the last century and a half the archeologists have found, in the ruins of ancient cities in Asia Minor, the evidence which proves the early existence of this Virgin Mother and her spontaneously generated and virgin born son Atys.

This record is not contained in scrolls forged by the priesthood, but is carved on stone monuments which even the ravages of time have not yet been able to efface.

Great Mother

The earliest record of Cybele and Atys is found in the land of the Hittites, the name of the race being written Heth in the Bible. They appear to have been among the more important racial elements in northern

Syria and southeastern Asia Minor for more than a thousand years, from about 2000 B.C. down to about 900 B.C.

In the mountainous region of the upper waters of the Sangarius, there exists numerous monuments of great antiquity, showing a style of marked individuality, and implying a high degree of artistic skill on the part of the people who produced them. On some of these monuments are engraved the names of "Midas the King," and the Goddess "Kybile the Mother." Even the title "king" appears to have been borrowed by the Greeks from this source.

These monuments are found in Lydia, Phrygia, Cappadocia, Lycaonia, and Syria, and indicate the existence of a homogeneous civilization in these countries at one time.

The ancient road from Pteria to Sardis crossed the upper Sangarius valley, and its old course may be traced by the monuments of this early period. Close to this ancient road, on a lofty plateau which overhangs the monument inscribed with the names of Midas and Kybile (Cybele), are the remains of a great city, surrounded by rock-sculptures, quite as remarkable as those of the Cappadocian city of Pteria.

The plateau is approximately two miles in circumference, and presents on all sides a perpendicular face of rock 50 to 200 feet high. This natural defense was crowned by a wall partly Cyclopean and partly built of large, squared stones, indicating that this city was evidently the center of the ancient Phrygian kingdom of the Sangarius valley.

Of the monuments existing around this city, two classes may be referred to the period of Phrygian greatness. That which is inscribed with the name "Midas the King" is the most remarkable example of one class, in which a large, perpendicular surface of rock is covered with geometrical patterns of squares, crosses and maeanders, surmounted by a pediment supported in the center by a pilaster in low relief. In some cases a floral pattern occupies part of the surface, and in one case the two sides of

Great Mother

the pediment are filled with two Sphinxes of archaic type.

In some of these monuments a door-way is carved in the lower part; the door usually being closed; but in the case of the Sphinx Monument just mentioned, the valves of the door are thrown wide open and permit access to a small chamber, on the back of which is sculptured in relief an image of the Mother-goddess Cybele, having on the side of her a lion which rests its forepaws on her shoulder and places its head against hers.

This may have a definite relation to Tarot Card No. 8, in which appears a picture which may be that of Cybele. The horizontal figure 8, the ancient occult number ascribed to Hermes, hovers over her head, indicating that she represents a cosmic principle. The woman is usually shown as closing the mouth of a lion, while in other pictures she is indicated as opening the lion's mouth.

The lion, as the king of beasts, signifies subhuman forces and expressions of the vital electricity. When the woman tames the lion, the symbolism means the conquest of man's animalistic nature, the great force that rules most human beings, to their detriment, as shown by Prof. Hotema in his work titled the Great Red Dragon mentioned in the Bible (Rev.12:3).

This is one of the strongest forces in Nature. It is devouring man by inches, sapping his vitality, shorting his lifespan, and pushing him into obscurity. The Ancient Masters waged a constant war against it.

Sometimes a grave has been found hidden behind the carved front in the lower part of these monuments. In others no grave can be detected, but it is probable that they are all sepulchral. The imitation of woodwork is obvious on several monuments of this kind.

The second class is marked by the heraldic type of two animals, usually lions rampant, facing each other, but divided by a pillar or some other device. This type is occasionally found conjoined with the preceding; and various details common to both classes show that there was no great difference in time between them.

The heraldic type is used on the monuments which appear to be the older, and the geometrical pattern is often employed on the inscribed monuments, which are obviously later than the earliest uninscribed. Monuments of this class are carved on the

front of a sepulchral chamber, the entrance to which is a small doorway placed high
and inaccessible in the rocks. There are also many rock monuments of the Roman era.

The chief "Hittite" site in Asia Minor is seen in the ruins of the immense pre-
historic and remarkable rock-sculptures near Boghaz Keui in Cappadocia, about 100
miles east of Angora. From this center the remains of ancient roads radiate toward
Syria and the Aegean Sea.

The remains of Boghaz Keui are indubitably pre-Persian and Pre-Greek. They con-
sist of a large fortified city on a steep slope, enclosed by two deep ravines, and
falling to northward over 800 feet from summit to base.

The acropolis was strengthened with a circle of stone redoubts, between which led
vary narrow gateways, and with internal redoubts as well.

Just inside of what seems to have been its principal center, is a rock face inscribed with nine lines of Hittite characters, greatly perished by the ravages of
time, and a similar inscription, equally illegible, can be detected on a neighboring
rock. Below the acropolis on the northeast is a residential quarter, containing large
ruins of what seems to have been a temple built round a central court. The whole
site is surrounded by a strong stone wall 14 feet thick, with towers about 100 feet

The monument which earliest rendered Boghaz Keui famous, is the sculptured rock
grotto, a mile to the east, called Yasili Kaya Here. Two peethral galleries are
adorned with reliefs in panel, the large gallery shewing two processions, which,
starting on both walls from the entrance, meet at the head of the grotto.

On the left wall are 45 figures, headed by a gigantic male figure, erect on the
bent necks of two men. On the right wall he is opposed by a female of practically
equal stature, standing on a lioness, and followed by a young male with battle-axe,
erect on a similar beast. Behind these are 20 figures of mitred priests, etc.

The female is the Goddess of Western Asia, the Great Mother of the Gods and of
all Men, attended by her virgin born son, Atys, "with whose help she creates the
world." Priests or minor divinities follow them.

Great Mother

The other procession, according to the analogy of other monuments, should be composed of mortals bearing "sacra" and headed by their king, who makes offering or dedicates his city to, or engages in some mystic union with, the Goddess and her Son. The figure following him seem to be that of his high priest. Hittite symbols are carved above many of the figures. Besides the processions, there are five independent reliefs in the gallery and its approach, one repeating the figure of the high priest.

H. Winchler, of the Berlin Oriental Society, was sent to examine the ruins and monuments, and he established the fact that Boghaz Keui was the capital of a powerful Hittite dynasty from 1500 B.C. to at least 1100 B.C. He says its ancient name was Hatti. At the height of its power, it ruled all Asia Minor, down to the Aegean and northern Syria to the headquarters of the Orontes, and was also overlord of the Mitanni and the Amurri in Mesopotamia.

The legends agree in locating the rise of the worship of the Great Mother in Asia Minor. Her best-known early seats of worship were Mt. Ida, Mt. Sipylus, Cyzicus, Sardis and Pessinus, the last-named city in Galatia near the borders of Roman Phrygia, finally becoming the strongest center of this worship. Cybele and Atys were later known to the Romans and Greeks as esentially Phrygian, and all Phrygia was spoken of as sacred to them.

From Asia Minor the worship of Cybele and Atys spread first to Greek territory, appearing in Thrace at an early date, and was known in Boeotia by the poet Pindar in the 6th century B.C., and entered Attica near the beginning of the 4th century B.C.

The Greeks from the first saw in the Great Mother a resemblance to their own Rhea, and finally identified the two completely. She came to be regarded in three aspects: Rhea, the Homeric and Hesiodic goddess of Cretan origin; the Phrygian Mother Cybele, with Atys; and the Greek Great Mother, a modified form of the Phrygian Mother, to be explained as the original Goddess of the Phrygians of Europe, communicated to the Greek stock before the Phrygian invasion of Asia Minor and the consequent mingling of the Asiatic stock.

In 204 B.C., in obedience to the Sibylline prophecy which said that whenever an enemy from abroad should make war on Italy, he could be expelled and conquered if the

-21-

Great Mother

Great Mother Cybele were brought to Rome. And so, the worship of Cybele, together
with her sacred symbol, a small meteoric stone reputed to have fallen from heaven,
were transferred to Rome and established in a temple on the Palatine.

Primarily, Cybele was a deification of the earth as reproducing and sustaining
the wild life of Nature; secondarily, she was the nourishing Mother of Man and the
giver of the arts of life. She was known as the All-begetter, the All-nourisher, the

Mother of all the Blest. She was the great, fruitful, kindly earth itself. She was

called the Mountain Mother, her sanctuaries almost invariable being upon mountains,
and frequently in caves, the name Cybele itself being by some derived from the latter.
Her priests, the Galli, were enuchs attired in female garb, with

long hair fragrant with ointment.

Like Aphrodite and Adonis in Syria, like Isis and Osiris in Egypt, Cybele and
Atys formed a duality which symbolized the relations between Mother Earth and her

Fruitage.

By the end of the Republic, the worship of Cybele and Atys had attained promi-
nence in Rome, and under the Empire it became one of the three most important cults
in the Roman world, the other two being those of Mithra and Isis. It came to an end
in 394 A.D. when it was outlawed by the Christian Emperor.

CHAPTER V

The Mysterious Resurrection

Why did all the leading races of the Ancient World have their Crucified and
Resurrected God?

The custom was not isolated, but general, and it symbolized a general principle
of Creation. That was its purpose, and that General Principle is the Immortality of
Life.

For six hundred years, said Cumont, the Romans worshipped Cybele and her Virgin
Born Son Atys.

That period extended from 204 B.C. until the practice was banned in 394 A.D. by
the Christian Emperor of the Roman Empire, in order to prohibit and prevent any and

Resurrection

all competition with the newly established religion called Christianity.

During those six hundred years, the Galli or eunuch priests, attired in female garb, with flowing hair fragrant with ointment, led the mourning celebrants each year

in solemn procession thru the streets of Rome, bearing aloft the emblem of a young man, nailed to a tree and wearing on his head a corwn of Violets, which was changed

to a Crown of Thorns in the case of Jesus (Mat.27:29, etc.).

Here we have the ancient picture of Atys, the only begotten Son and Savior of the world, born of Cybele, the Great Mother of the Gods says the uncensored dictionaries and encyclopedias; and this Great Mother was only

a symbol of the zodiacal sign Virgo the Virgin; and the Son and Savior Atys was "dead."

But on the third day, the mourning turned to a great festival of joy, for ATYS HAD RISEN FROM THE DEAD. And at that moment the happy devotees of Atys shouted:

"Death is swallowed up in victory. O Death, where is thy string? O Grave, where is thy victory?"--Isa. 25:8; 1 Cor. 15:54,55.

As the Ancient World gives up its secrets to the diligent researchers, more of the fraudulent work of the Pious Church Fathers is exposed.

The time of the year of this celebration was early spring, when violets bloomed and all Nature was RESURRECTING from winter sleep (death).

"The dead are rising to life," said the Astrologers, and the people rejoiced and celebrated. This important event was symbolized in their Zodiac,

and that's the chief reason why the Mother Church hates Astrology.

The solemn ceremony began at the Vernal Equinox, on March 22. The next day was the day the priests blew their sacred trumpets with a loud

blast, to call the faithful. March 24th was the "Day Of Blood." As Atys bled the day he was "crucified," so must the priests bleed now to honor him. So the high priest drew blood from his arm and presented it as an humble offering.

Then the drums thundered and howls of compassion pierced the air. And the priest frenziedly gashed themselves in the excitement until blood flowed to their feet.

What fools religion makes of the mind-conditioned mob. And the Church Fathers put the event in their Bible, to the effect

that "Without shedding of blood is no remission" (Isa.4:4; Heb.9:22).

Primarily and fundamentally, the celebration marked the annual Resurrection of the Sun God or Solar God from the Winter Solstice. With it there

came the Resurrection of the grass and flowers, and naked forests turned green with New Life. "All Nature rose from the dead," said the Astrologers.

Resurrection

And here we are, in the very heart of the carefully guarded secret of the Crucifixion and Resurrection of Gods.

This annual event was celebrated by all leading countries of antiquity, extending so far back that all traces of its origin are lost in the night of time.

It was celebrated in the case of Cybele and Atys four thousand years before the birth of Christianity. And when Christianity was established, Cybele became Mary and Atys became Jesus.

The original and direct purpose of the dramatic celebration of the fictitious Crucifixion and Resurrection of Gods was not to deceive the people into the belief that this process "washed us from our sins," as the biblical makers put it in their

Bible (Rev.1:5).

It was not for the purpose of presenting a Savior "which taketh away the sins of the world" (John 1:29).

It was designed as a standing commemoration to notice, honor and celebrate the mysterious process of Creation which reveals to man the Gateway to the Future Life.

It was to teach the Cosmic Cycle of Life, the Law of Cyclic Manifestation, the Law of Creation, which Wise Men of the Ancient World discovered and observed in the teaching of their followers the inspiring lesson,

that Death is far from being what it seems to be in this changing world of illusion.

They discovered that the Cosmic Cycle of Creation is presented in the case of invisible vapor which becomes water, then ice, and returns again as vapor to the in-

visible world, NOT IN EXTINCTION BUT IN SUSPENSION, potentially existing, ready to return to the visible world when the condition for such return are suitable and favorable.

In the world of illusion where all visible objects and bodies are constantly changing, and where men live by sight, they see not what they think they see; and

that is the reason why the Ancient Masters invented and presented the fable of the Crucified and Resurrected God. It was to teach man that Life, as well as vapor, also travels in a cycle.

The Mama Mater Cybele symbolized Mother Earth, and she is presented in Card 3 of the ancient Tarot as The Empress. She was a Nature Goddess; and her spontaneously generated and virgin born son Atys symbolized

Natural Phenomena, the visible products of Creation.

Prof. Cumont said in his book, "We can trace each phase of the transformation that changed it (this system) in the course of time from a collection of very primi-

tive Nature Beliefs (Nature Worship) into a (fraudulent) system of spiritualized mysteries." Yes; and who did that? The cunning priesthood.

T. W. Doane wrote: "If we wish to find the gods and goddesses of the ancestors

-24-

Resurrection

of mankind, we must look to the sun, the moon, the stars, the sky, the earth, the sea, the dawn, the clouds, the wind, etc., which the ancient races personified and worshipped" (Bible Myths, p.468).

In his book "The World's Sixteen Crucified Saviors," Graves said that Christianity is nothing more than the latest version of these fictitious Crucified and Resurrected Gods.

Eusebius of Caesarea, the pagan bishop who did more than any one else in the struggle at Nicea in the 4th century to establish the Roman Catholic Church, admitted in his History of Christianity, that there is nothing esentially new about it.

And the pagan Apollonius who became the Paul of the Epistles in the Bible, declared that the gospel which he preached, had been "preached (by the Ancient Pagan Masters) to every creature which is under heaven, whereof I Paul am made a minister" (Col.1:23).

The Bible Decoded

CHAPTER VI

Birth of Gods

It is in order to state at this point that we are not engaged in the task of presenting a postulate for argument, but in decoding certain allegories of the Bible for enlightenment. It is more proper to say that we are decoding certain fables and symbols of the ancient scrolls from which the Bible was compiled by the Church Fathers

This work of ours deals directly with the ancient Doctrine of the Future Life, and it is our purpose to surprise and shock the Christian World by definitely showing, that the Doctrine under consideration was concealed from the corrupting eyes of the world by the Masters of the Sacred Wisdom in the symbolism of a Crucified and Resurrected god or savior. However, before the god or savior could be crucified and resurrected, he must first be born in the physical world; and it is that phase of our subject which we shall now proceed to notice.

The Bible Decoded

In one of the most elaborate and remarkable works on mythology ever produced, Charles Francois Dupuis shows in his "Origin Of Worship," that all the religious systems of the world, including Christianity, were derived chiefly from Solar Worship.

All the solar deities, he said, have a common history, which summarized, is substantially as follows:

"The god is born about December 25th, without sexual intercourse, for the Sun, entering the winter solstice, emerges in the sign of Virgo, the heavenly Virgin. His mother remains ever-virgin, since the rays of the Sun, passing thru the zodiacal sign, leave it intact.

"His infancy is begirt with dangers, because the new-born Sun is feeble in the midst of the winter's fogs and mists, which threaten to devour him. His life is one of toil and peril, culminating at the vernal equinox in a final struggle with the powers of darkness.

"At that period, the days and night are of equal length, and both day and night fight for the mastery. Tho the night veils the Sun and he seems dead; tho he has descended out of sight, below the earth, yet he rises again triumphant, and he rises in the sign of the Lamb, and is thus the Lamb of God, carrying away the darkness and death (sins of the world--Jn.1:29) of the winter months.

"Henceforth he triumphs, growing ever stronger and brighter. He ascends into the zenith, and there he glows, on the right hand of God, himself God, the very substance of the Father, the brightness of his glory, and the express image of his person, upholding all things by his life-giving power."

Dr. G. W. Brown, author of "Researches in Oriental History," said: "Strange as it may seem, whilst Atys, Mithra, Osiris, Dionysos, Bacchus, Apollo, Serapis, with many others, including Christ, in name, all masculine sun gods, and all interblended, a knowledge of one is generally a knowledge of the whole, wherever located or worshipped."

That being the case, we shall relate the story of the god, the Son of God, the Lamb of God, by excerptions from the great work of T. W. Doane, titled Bible Myths, copyright 1910:--

The history of Christ Jesus, the Christian Savior, "the true Light, which lighteth every man that cometh into the world" (Jn.1:9), is simply a history of the Sun.

1. The birth of Christ Jesus is said to have occured at early dawn, on December 25th, and the Christian ceremonies of the Nativity are celebrated, even at this time, in Bethlehem and Rome very early in the morning.

This is the Sun's birthday, and this was the beginning of the New Year and was celebrated as such in the ancient world. But the Church Fathers changed this, to hide the fact that Jesus was just a mythical Sun God, by moving the date of the New Year up seven days, and calling December 25th Christ-mas.

On the first moment after midnight on December 24th, all the ancient nations of the earth, as if by common consent, celebrated the accouchement of the "Queen of Heaven," the "Celestial Virgin," and the birth of the god Sol.

Birth of Gods

On that day the Sun having fully entered the winter solstice, the zodiacal Sign of the Virgin was rising on the eastern horizon. The female symbol of this stellar sign was represented first by ears of corn, then with a new-born male child in the woman's arms.

Such was the picture of the Persian sphere cited by Aben-Ezra: "The division of the first decan of the Virgin represents a Virgin with flowing hair, sitting in a chair, with two ears of corn in her hand, and suckling an infant called Jesus by some nations, and Christ in Greek."

This denotes the Sun, which, at the moment of the winter solstice, precisely when the Persian Magi drew the horoscope of the New Year, was placed on the bosom of the Virgin, rising heliacally in the eastern horizon. On this account the Sun was figured in their astrological pictures under the form of a child suckled by a chaste Virgin.

Thus we observe that Christ Jesus was born on the same day as Atys, Mithra, Buddha, Bacchus, Adonis, Osiris, Horus, Hercules, and other personifications of the Sun.

Rt. Rev. Wm. M. Brown, D.D., of the Protestant Episcopal Church of Galion, Ohio, shows in his book titled Science & History, how the Mother Church grew rich and powerful, and made millions of slaves, by historicalizing the ancient myth of the Sun God. He said:

"Suppose you had been a child living in Rome a few years before Jesus is supposed to have been born. About a week before December 25th you would have seen people preparing for a great feast, just as they do today in Europe.

"To those Romans, December 25th was the birthday of the Sun. They wrote that in gold letters in their calendars. Every year, at that time, the Sun was born, and that would end the darkness and misery of winter. So they had a great feast, with presents for all, for the best day of all was December 25th.

"That feast, they would tell you, was thousands of years old.

"And just outside of Rome was an underground temple of the Phrygian Sun God Atys. At midnight, the first minute of December 25th, you would have seen that temple lighted with candles, and priests in white garments at the altar, and boys burning incense, exactly as you see today in the Roman Catholic Church at midnight on December 24th.

"And the worshippers of Atys would have told you that he was a God who came from heaven to be born as a man and to redeem men from their sins; and he was born in a dark cave or stable on December 25th, just as the gospels present Jesus hundreds of years later.

"Then suppose you had gone to the temple in Rome where the Egyptians worshipped, and there you would have seen them also celebrating the birth of their god Horus, who was born of a Virgin in a stable on December 25th.

"In their temple you would see a statue or figure of the infant-god Horus lying in a manger, and a statue of his Virgin Mother Isis standing beside it; just as in a Roman Catholic Church on Christmas day you find a stable or cave rigged up and the infant Jesus in a manger and a figure of Mary beside it.

-27-

Birth of gods

"Then you might go to the Greek Temple and find the Greeks paying respect to the figure of their savior-god in a manager.

"And if you visited the quarters of the gladiators, the war-captives from Germany, you would find them also holding a feast, and they would explain that December 25th, all over Europe, was the great feast of Yule, or the Wheel, which means that the Sun had turned back, like a wheel, and was going once more to redeem humanity from the Hell of Winter in the Heaven of Summer" (pp.138-9).

2. Christ Jesus was born of a Virgin. This Virgin, of whom is born the Sun, the true Savior of Mankind, has three aspects: The bright Dawn, the dark Earth, or the desky Night.

This Celestial Virgin was feigned to be a mother. She is represented in the Indian Zodiac with ears of corn in one hand, and the lotus in the other. In Kircher's Zodiac of Hermes, she has corn in both hands. In other planispheres of the Egyptians she carries ears of corn in one hand, and the infant Savior Horus in the other. In Roman Catholic countries, she is generally represented with the child in one hand, and the lotus or lily in the other.

The poets of the Veda indulged freely in theogonic speculations without fear of any contradictions. They knew of Indra as the greatest of gods, they knew of Agni as the god of gods, they knew of Vsruna as the ruler of all, and they were by no means startled at the idea that their Indra had a mother, or that Varuna was nursed in the lap of Aditi, the Dawn. All this was true to nature; for their god was the Sun, and the mother who bore and nursed him was the Dawn.

Cox wrote: "With scarcely an exception, all the names by which the Virgin goddess was known point to this mythology of the Dawn" (Aryan Myths, vol.i, p.228).

In the Vishnu Purana, Devaki, the virgin mother of the Hindu Savior Chrishna, is called Aditi, which is the name of the Dawn. Devaki is Aditi, Aditi is the Dawn, and Dawn is the Virgin Mother. The Savior of mankind who is born of her, the Dawn is the Sun, and the Sun is Chrishna, and Chrishna is Christ.

3. The birth of Jesus was foretold by a star. A glance at the geography of the sky will show the "chaste, pure, immaculate Virgin, suckling her infant," preceded by a Star, which rises immediately preceding the Virgin and her child. This was "his Star" which informed the "Wise Men," the "Magi," the Astrologers and Sun worshippers, and "the shepherds who watched their flocks by night" that the Savior of Mankind was about to be born.

4. The heavenly Host sang praises. All Nature smiles at the birth of the Sun. "To him all angels cry aloud, the heavens, and all the powers therein."

5. He was visited by the Magi. This was the regular practice, for the Magi were Sun Worshippers, and at early dawn on December 25th, the Astrologers of the Hittites, the Phrygians, the Chaldeans, the Arabs, and other Oriental nations, greeted the infant Savior with gold, frankincense and myrr.

These races started to salute their God long before daylight, and having ascended a high mountain, they anxiously waited for his birth, facing the East, and there hailed the Sun's first rays with incense and prayer. The shepers also, watching their flocks by night, were in the habit of prostrating themselves, and paying homage to their god, the Sun.

6. He was born in a Cave. The narrative of Christ Jesus corresponds with that of the other Sun gods and Saviors. They are nearly all represented as being born in a cave or dungeon.

This is the dark abode from which the Sun rises in the morning. As the Dawn springs fully armed from the forehead of the cloven Sky, so the eye first discerns the blue of heaven, as the first faint arch of light is seen in the East. This arch is the cave in which the infant is nourished until he reaches his full strength—in other words, until the light of day has fully come.

As the hour of his birth drew near, the mother became more beautiful, her form more brilliant, while the dungeon was filled with a heavenly light, as when Zeus came to Danae in the golden shower.

When Christ Jesus was born, on a sudden there was a great light in the cave, so their eyes could not bear it (Protevangelion, Apoc. Ch. 14).

7. He was ordered to be put to death. All the Sun Gods are fated to bring ruin upon their parents or the reigning monarch. For this reason, they attempt to prevent his birth, and failing in this, seek to destroy him when born. Who is the dark, wicked Kansa, or his counterpart Herod? He is Night, who reigns supreme, but who must lose his power when the young prince of glory, the Invincible, is born.

The Sun scatters the Darkness; and so the phrase went out that the child was to be the destroyer of the reigning monarch, or his parent, Night; and oracles, and magi it was said, warned the latter of the doom which would overtake him. The newly-born babe is therefore ordered to be put to death by the sword, or exposed to the bare hillside, as the Sun seems to rest on the Earth (Ida) at its rising.

And so, the angel of the Lord appeared to Joseph in a dream, saying, Arise, and take the young child and his mother, and flee into Egypt, and be thou there until I bring thee word: For Herod will seek the young child to destroy him (Mat.2:13)

8. He was tempted by the devil. The temptation by, and victory over, the evil one, whether Mara or Satan, is the victory of the Sun over the clouds of storm and darkness.

Growing up in obscurity, the time comes when he makes himself known, tries himself in his first struggle with his gloomy foes, and shines without a rival. He is rife for his destined mission, but is met by the demon of storm, who disputes with him in the duel of the storm.

In this struggle against darkness and storm, the beneficent hero remains the conqueror, and the gloomy army of Mara, or Satan, is broken, rent and scattered.

Free from every obstacle and from every adversary, the Sun sets in motion across boundless space his disk with a thousand rays, having avenged the attempts of his foe. He appears then in all his glory; the god has attained the summit of his course, it is the moment of triumph.

9. He was put to death on the cross. The Sun has run its course and moved back to his extreme southern limit in the winter solstice. His career is ended, and he is at last overcome by his enemies. The powers of darkness, and of winter, which had

Birth of gods

battled with him, have at length won the victory.

The glorious Sun of summer is finally slain, crucified in the heavens, and pierced by the arrow, spear or thorn of winter. It was in the winter solstice that the ancients wept for Atys, Adonis, Tammuz, and the other Sun gods, who were put to death by the thorn of winter.

Before he dies, the Sun sees all his disciples, his retinue of light, and the twelve hours of the day, and the twelve months of the year, and the twelve signs of the Zodiac, all disappear in the sanguinary melee of the clouds of the approaching darkness.

These things must be. The suffering of a violent death was a necessary part of the mythos; and, when his hour had come, he must meet his doom, as surely as the Sun, once risen, must go across the sky, and then sink down into his bed beneath earth or sea. It was an iron fate from which there was no escape.

And so, the gospel scribe makes his Jesus say, "But for this cause came I unto this hour" (Jn.12:27). "From this time forth began Jesus to show unto his disciples how that he must go unto Jerusalem, and suffer many things of the elders and chief priests and scribes, and be killed, and be raised again the third day" (Mat.16:21, etc.).

10. And women were there beholding afar off. The ever-faithful woman who is always near at the death of the Sun god, is "the fair and tender light which sends its soft hue over the Eastern sky as the Sun sinks in death beneath the Western waters.

At the death of the Sun god Hercules, Iole, the fair-haired Dawn, stands near, cheering him to the last. With her gentle hands she sought to sooth his dying-pain, and with pitying words to cheer him in his woe. Then once more the face of Hercules flushed with joy, and he said:

"Ah, Iole, brightest of maidens, thy voice shall cheer me as I sink down in the sleep of death. I saw and loved thee in the bright morning time, and now again thou has come, in the evening, fair as the soft clouds which float around the dying Sun."

The dark mists were spreading over the glowing sky, but still Hercules sought to gaze on the fair face of Iole, and to comfort her in her sorrow for him He said,

"Weep not, Iole, my toil is done, and now is the time for rest. I shall see thee again in the bright land which is never trodden by the dark feet of night."

The same story is related in the legend of all the Sun gods. In the case of Apollo, the bright Dawn, from whom he had parted in the early part of his career, comes to his side at eventide, and again meets him when his journey has almost come to an end.

The faithful women "also bewailed and lamented" Jesus, and to them he said these words:

"Daughter of Jerusalem, weep not for me, but weep for yourselves and for your children" (Luke 23:28).

There is no greater proof of the universal adoration paid by the ancient races to the Sun, the Stars, and the Constellations, than the arrangement of the Hebrew

Birth of gods

Camp in the Desert, and the allegory relating to the Twelve Signs of the Zodiac as the Twelve Tribes of Israel, ascribed in the Hebrew legends to Jacob, who represented the Zodiac.

The Camp was a quadrilateral, in sixteen divisions, of which the central four were occupied by symbols of the sacred four elements, fire, air, water and earth.

The four divisions at the four angles of the quadrilateral exhibited the four zodiacal signs which the astrologers called the Fixed Signs, and which they regarded as subject to the influence of the four great Royal Stars, Regulus in Leo, Aldebaran in Taurus, Antares in Scorpio, and Fomalhaut in Pisces, on which falls the water poured out by Aquarius. Of these Constellations the Scorpion was represented in the Hebrew Blazonry by the Celestial Eagle, the Wings of the Sphinx, and the Eagle rises at the same time with it and is its paranatellon. The other signs were arranged on the four faces of the quadrilateral, and in the parallel and interior divisions.

The Vernal and Autumnal Equinoxes the Astrologers called the Gates of Heaven. And they lamented when, after the Autumnal Equinox, they saw the malign influence of the venomous Scorpion, the vindictive Archer, and the filthy He-Goat "drag" the sun down toward the Winter Solstice.

Arriving there, they said that the Sun had been slain and gone to the realm of darkness.

Remaining there for three days, the Sun rose again, and ascended northward in the heavens, to redeem the earth from the cold, gloom and darkness of winter, which was emblematical of evil and suffering, as the Spring, Summer and Autumn were emblems of happiness and immortality.

11. He descended into hell. This, as we have shown, is the sun's descent into the Winter Solstice. It enters the sign of Capricornus, or the Goat, and the astronomical winter begins. The days have reached their shortest span, and the Sun has reached its extreme southern limit. The Winter Solstice reigns, and the Sun seems to stand still. For three days and three nights the Sun remains in "hell" (the lower regions.)

12. He rose again from the dead and ascended into heaven. Jesus said, "Destroy this temple, and in three days I will raise it up (Jn.2:19).

The resurrection from the dead, and the ascension into heaven, are in general acknowledged to be solar features, as the history of the solar heros agree in this particular.

At the Winter Solstice the ancients wept and mourned for the Sun gods, done to death by the sword of winter,--and on the third day they rejoiced at the Resurrection of their Lord of Light and Life.

With their usual schemes, the Mother Church endeavored to give a Christian significance to the rites which the Church borrowed from paganism and in this case, the mourning for Atys, Adonis, Tammuz, Osiris, etc., became the mourning for Jesus, and then joy at the rising of the Sun became the joy at the rising of the "Son of Righteousness," at the Resurrection of Jesus.

The festival of the Resurrection was usually held by the ancients on March 25th, when the Spring Season produced the Resurrection of the grass and flowers, and dormant forests turned green with new life. All Nature was "rising from the dead," said the Astrologers.

Was Man ruled by the same law? Did he "rise from the dead"? Does Universal Law have exceptions?

Exceptions belong to the realm of speculation. Mathematicians do not record exceptions. Mechanical laws know no exceptions. In a word, Universal Laws are invariable, comnipresent, illustrative of the character of Creative Processes.

Solar Worship

While the devotees in general fail to recognize it, yet their religious system, not only in its external form but in its very essence, is a survival of the Nature Worship of the Ancient World, in which the Sun was the Most High God and the Consuming Fire (Heb.12:29).

The Sun was properly recognized as the Generative Power of the Universe. He overshadows the receptive Earth with his Animative Rays and all living forms appear. M. Soury said:

"Amid all these forces, the mightiest is, without question, the Sun, the Fire of Heaven, and the supreme cause of life on our planet. The very Life Blood of our Celestial Father flows in the veins of Mother Earth. We are the Children of the Sun in fact as well as in fiction. But all the terrestrial life, all the warmth and all the light, are the effluents of the Sun" (Religion of Israel, pp.3,4).

John Newton, M.R.C.S., of England said: "The glorious Sun, the God of this World, the Source of Light and Life on our earth,, was early adored by humanity, and an effigy thereof used as a symbol.

"Mankind watched with rapture its rays gain strength daily in the spring, until the golden glories of midsummer had arrived, when the earth was bathed in his beams during the longest days, which ripened the fruit and grain that his returning course from the Winter Solstice had brought into life.

"When the Sun once more began his course downward to the Winter Solstice, his voraties sorrowed, for he seemed to sicken and grow paler at the advent of winter, when his weakened rays feebly reached the earth, and all Nature, benumed and cold, sank into a death-like sleep.

"And so, feasts were instituted and fests were celebrated to honor the beginning of the various phases of the Solar Year; and these have continued from the earliest known period, under various names, down to our own days" (The Assyrian Grove).

The leading deities in the pantheons of the ancient gods were Solar Deities, among which were Chrishna, Vishnu, Osiris, Atys, Mithra, Apollo, Hercules, Adonis, Baal and Bacchus. They were all Solar Gods.

Many of the fables concerning Moses, Joshua, Jonah and other biblical characters, are solar myths. Samson and Hercules were Solar Gods, and St. Augustine declared that they were one and the same under different names.

CHAPTER VII

L I G H T

A mysterious Book with Seven Seals is mentioned in the Bible (Rev. 5). That refers to Man.

A strong angel proclaimed with a loud voice, Who is worthy to open the book, and to loose the seals thereof? And I wept much, because no man was found worthy to open and to read the book, neither to look thereon.

What do we know about Life? What do we know about the constitution of Man? He is the greatest mystery in Creation and modern science knows less about him than the Ancient Masters did five thousand years ago.

We here stand at the first door of that great school of the Masters, known as the Ancient Mysteries; and the Candidate has been prepared, tested and found worthy for the great event of his life. He is going to be taught the mystery of his Body and the Secret of his Soul.

This Candidate is mentioned in the Bible as the Lamb, and when he opened one of the Seven Seals, "I heard, as it were, the noise of thunder, and one of the four beasts saying, Come and See.

"And I saw, and behold a white horse; and he that sat on him had a bow; and a crown was given to him; and he went forth conquering, and to conquer (Rev. 6;1,2).

"And I saw heaven opened, and behold a white horse; and he that sat upon him was called Faithful and True, and in righteousness he doth judge and make war.

"His eyes were as a flame of fire, and on his Head were many crowns; and he had a name written, that no man knew but himself. And he was clothed with a vesture" dyed red, and his name is called the Son Of Light (Rev.19:11-13).

Initiation in the Ancient Mysteries transformed the "man of darkness" to the Son Of Light. Let us proceed:

The angel that talked with me came again, and waked me, as a man that is wakened out of his sleep, and he said unto me, What seest thou?

And I said, I have looked, and behold a candlestick all of gold (spinal cord), with bowl on top of it (brain), and seven lamps (major nerve centers of the body); and two olive trees by it, one upon the right side and the other on the left side.

Then I answered and spake to the angel that talked with me, saying, What are these two olive trees upon the right and left side of the candlestick, thru which the two golden pipes empty the golden oil out of themselves.

And he answered me and said, These are the two anointed ones, that stand by the Lord of the whole earth (Zechariah, Chap. 4).

The two olive trees are the two serpents of the Caduceus, and they are the two golden pipes that empty the creative essence, generated at the base of the spine and,

when not consumed in fornication, is carried up to the "bowl" on top of the golden
candlestick, where it served to increase man's mental power and his state of consciousness.

And who is the Lord of the whole earth? He is the Son Of Light who has been
instructed by the Masters in the mysteries of Life and taught the nature of his Body
and the Secret of his Soul.

Then the Roman Catholic Church was established, and the Sacred Wisdom of the
Masters was outlawed, and the Masters were silenced and murdered.

The Church Fathers knew that intelligent, enlightened people could not be enslaved nor
frightened by a fictitious god.

Within a century after Constantine founded the Church as a political movement,
classical antiquity came to an inglorious end, and the gloomy Dark Ages began to
settle over the Roman Empire. It soon sank into black oblivion, and so remained for
a thousand years.

Then the courageous Martin Luther rose up out of this darkness in the 16th century, and nailed his damning theses to the church door. That was the dawn of a New
Age. Other men of courage, inspired by Luther's work, rose up and looked for Light;
and that was the birth of Protestantism.

And then began the bloody struggle of the Church to hold its power and to eradi-
cate "heresy" and Protestantism. But the Dawning Light of Knowledge carried
Protestantism on to victory, and the Sun of Science began to rise in the Land of
Darkness.

The Darkness lifted as learning advanced, and intelligent critics began to examine the Holy Bible, to take it apart, and to expose its true nature. They showed
that the Word Of God was based on ancient Astrology and Mythology, but falsely presented by the Church as history. They further showed that the Twelve Tribes of
Israel were nothing more than the Twelve Constellations of the Zodiac, yet presented
by the Church as a race of people. And, more amazing, they discovered that the

gospel Jesus was a mythical, fraudulent personification of the Sun and also the head sign of the Zodiac, the Ram, and old Lamb.

Bibliolatry

Bibliolatry is a blind, superstitious worship of the Bible as the Divinely Inspired Word of a mythical God in the sky, based not upon any knowledge of the Bible, but upon the fraudulent claim of the Church that the Bible is a direct relation of that God.

We do not teach our children, as we should, that the world has two classes of men:--Intelligent men without religion, and religious men without intelligence.

We neglect to teach our children that nearly all the Founding Fathers of this country were Agnostics who fled from England to escape from the rule and power of the Church.

Nor do we teach them, as we should, that the thousands of "disbelievers" include the leading men of the world, such as Bruno, Galileo, Copernicus, Socrates, Voltaire, Humboldt, Burbank, Webster, Einstein, Washington, Franklin, Jefferson, Lincoln, Edison Carnegie, Taft, Shaw, Brisbane, LordBryon, Thomas Carlyle, Thomas Paine, Joseph Mc Cade, Chapman Cohen, Omar, Silensins, Comte, Mark Twain, Emerson, Dickens, Gandhi, Holmes, Hubbard, Hughes, Hugo, Ingersoll, Kipling, Lowell, Mill, Mozart, Napoleon, Poe, Shakespeare, Spencer, Sinclair, Wells,--to name a few of them.

Most of us are taught in our youth to regard the Bible as a sacred Book, as one containing an authoritative revelation of a God in the sky on the creation of the world, and the history, duty, and destiny of man. We are taught to accept strange, unreasonable and miraculous stories in the Bible as true--because they are in the Bible.

We grow up, taking it for granted that Moses, Abraham, Isaac, Jacob and the Children of Israel were real persons; that the history of the Hebrews is faithfully reported in the Old Testament; that the "prophets" wrote the books attributed to them

Bible decoded
 Light

that Jesus Christ was born at Bethlehem on the first Christmas Day more than 1950

years ago, and crucified on the first Good Friday about 33 years later; that he rose

from the dead in three days, and "ascended up to heaven"; that the Apostles and

Evangelists wrote the books which bear their names; and that these are the reason

why there is a Bible and a Christian Church today.

During the many centuries that the Church possessed almost unlimited power, any

one who studied the Bible or questioned its "holy authority," was either hacked to

pieces or burned to cinders. Even now, challengers are persecuted as much as public

opinion and the law will allow.

Few people today know that "it is a matter of history," wrote Mangasarian, "that

in the name of this Jewish-Christian volume, which people do not read and are but

superficially acquainted with, a hundred million lives in Europe alone were destroyed

(The Neglected Book, p.14).

And it is not generally known that for a thousand years, roughly from 500 to

1500 A.D., the educational systems of Europe were ruled by the Church and conducted
by the prejudiced priesthood, and the only textbook in use was the Bible.

Life Cycle

Before the awakening that occurred during the Glorious Nineteenth Century, if a

person attempted to investigate the background of the Bible and report his findings,

his life was in imminent danger. He was denounced by the Mother Church as an enemy

of God and, as such, deserving of death. The prejudiced, mind-conditioned mob quick-

ly disposed of him, and "the Church was not responsible for what the mob did."

With the beginning of the Grand Nineteenth Century, the vast power which the

Church had so ruthlessly wielded for a thousand years, declined to where it was safer

for one to question the Bible. This has resulted in an enormous amound of amazing

Life Cycle

light being cast by unprejudiced researchers upon the ruins of the ancient world and
upon the Bible.

Until the great enlightenment which occurred in the Nineteenth Century, the
hieroglyphics of Egypt and the cuneiform inscriptions on the stone monuments thruout
Babylonia, Assyria, and Asia Minor in general, were undecipherable and not understood,
and the Bible was our sole authority for the history of Man and the ancient world
prior to the rise of Greek civilization.

Then in 1799 the trench digger's pick struck the Rosetta Stone in the loamy
soil of the Nile delta, releasing the voice of a long-voiceless past to refuse nearly
every one of Christianity's historical claims with a withering negative.

And even with the literature of ancient Egypt standing in translation as the
result of Champollion's marvelous work in deciphering the cryptic hieroglyphics of
the Egyptian monuments, the Mysterious Sphinx Riddle might again have been lost for
ages had not one man lifted the veil of Isis and revealed at last the Living Heart of
the Ancient Mysteries.

This language proved to be the open sesame to comprehension of that sacred,
esoterical, spiritual, as distinct from the superficial, literal meaning of the
Ancient Scriptures. It was, therefore, the lost Key to the Secret Meaning of the
Sacred Wisdom of the Ancient Masters; and its discovery ends almost two thousand years
of religious dupery, superstition, fanaticism, horrendous period of the Dark Ages, and
ushers in a new era of enlightenment, sanity and knowledge that are the supreme turning points in the eons of history.

Scholars have failed for two thousand years because they were caught and deceived by a clever trick of the Ancient Masters who wrote the Scriptures in symbol and
allegory to conceal the Sacred Wisdom. They wrote the Arcane Scripts in such a way
that they carried two separate and distinct meanings,--one designed for the masses
and the other for the Initiates and Disciples.

For two millennia the Bible has yielded nothing but bafflement and folly, because the secret code key to the symbolic language, in which it had been deftly written

-37-

Life Cycle

had been lost. In supreme ignorance and fear, the Mother Church ruthlessly crushed
every effort of a few discerning minds to recover the lost key.

With the amazing discoveries by the archeologists of the key to the ancient
hieroglyphics and cuneiform inscriptions on stone tablets and monuments, was revealed
the surprising existence of highly-developed civilizations long before the time previously assigned, on the authority of the misleading bibical genealogies, to the
creation of Man and his accomplishments.

And furthermore, these discoveries made possible the reconstruction with a great
degree of accuracy, the history of the ancient civilizations during the period to which
the Bible relates. While there are points of agreement between the biblical record
and the ancient monuments, there are many highly important points where the ancient
messages cut in stone and now understood, not only fail to confirm the biblical re-
cords, but flatly contradict them.

One of the biggest surprises that resulted from the discoveries of the researches,
was the evidence that at a period so remote as to be contemporary with the times in-
corrigibly listed by historians as "primitive," the Ancient Masters possessed scrolls
of such exalted Light and intellectual Wisdom as to lie beyond the comprehension of
vaunted modern science.

The time has come when modern pride must face the facts, that these supposedly
primitive people possesses scrolls which, by no possibility, could have been the product of "primitive" intellectuality.

Ancient scrolls which only ancient sages could have produced, bespeak the presence of sages on the scene. For men are known by their fruits.

The presence of sapient writings, the evidence of lost arts, the crumbling remains of edifices surpassing all present achievements--these are the things which
attest incontrovertibly to the existence of Intellectual Giants in "primitive" times.

We know now that what the ancient scrolls contained were the outlines of ancient
tradition and legend, formulated by the accumulated wisdom of ancient sages, covering
the observations and experiences of mankind for hundreds of thousands of years.

Out of that accumulated wisdom there came forth those set formulations of cosmic data, of cosmic laws, and of moral codes that have survived the test of time, and still stand as scientific commitments of the highest order.

The marvelous data which have come down to us in the form of fable, fiction, parable, allegory, symbol and dramatic poetry, present the substantial facts of Life and Creation, collected and correlated by ancient sages of the highest type.

And furthermore, the work in its entirely is so profound, that sixteen hundred years of the most consecrated effort of modern scholars to fathom it, has left its esoteric message still unrevealed.

But with the aid of the recent discoveries and of increasing knowledge, the persistent workers and unprejudiced researchers are slowly tearing the deceptive mask of literary disguises from the face of the Sacred Scriptures.

And it comes as a startling surprise for us to discover, that what has been gratuitously assumed to be the product of primitive naivete and heathenish supertition, is now seen to be the variegated cloak of a recondite wisdom.

Not only do the ridiculous symbols and ludicrous allegories bear the impress of genius competent to portray cosmic facts in cosmic figures and foolish fables, but these ancient authors register an equal skill in their artful concealment.

The employment by the ancient sages of the crafty disguise, has carried them so far beyond us in knowledge and skill, that we have been gulled into accepting the disguise for the real thing. Well, that is, under the persuasion of the priesthood, with the bitter alternative of burning for doubting.

With soft touches and deft strokes did the ancient wise men weave their profound pattern of celestial and terrestrial life, of astral powers and physical phenomena, thru their clever narratives of gods, saviors, men, mermaids, harpies, satyrs, centaurs, sphinxes, serpents, stage, dragons, boars, bulls, of labyrinths, mountains, seas, rivers, whirlwinds, clouds of fire and falling stars, that not one of the most outlandish details of their fabrications can be ignored, without the loss of some signal link of meaning.

Generations of scholars, chained for a thousand years in the cave of theological darkness, have perennially scoffed the suggestion that the ancient myths might be fanciful portrayals of esoteric facts.

These scholars of darkness have changed the Assyrians, Babylonians, Chaldeans, Egyptians and Greeks, the most enlightened races known in history, with possessing the mentality of immature children.

We have accused them of accepting for definite actualities their fire-breathing dragons, beasts with seven heads and ten horns, their griffins, maiads, Cyclops, Circes and Medusa's, their crucified gods and resurrected saviors, their men in a furnace and in the belly of a whale.

Referring to these matters, Dr. Alvin B. Kuhn said: "They (ancient sages) never dreamed that there would come an age so far lost in the mythical intent of their writings, as to suppose they ever meant literally what they said (allegorically). They could not have known that the wisest savants of a distant epoch would be so blinded by the forces of obscurantism as not to realize that the old books spoke only in terms of those earthly forms that adumbrate spiritual realities. The old masters of cosmic science were not in the habit of speaking 'precisely'; they spoke under the forms of figure always. They could not suspect that their indirect poetical (and allegorical) method would so outrageously befuddle modern 'intelligence'" (The Lost Light, p.86).

History informs us that after the birth of the Roman Catholic Church in the 4th century A.D., and the compilation of the Bible by the Church Fathers, the Church engaged in a systematic and ruthless campaign of destruction of the "old philosophy and literature of the heathens." The great Alexandrian Library, comprising 700,000 scrolls and manuscripts of the "superstitious heathens", was stormed and burned in 381 A.D. by a mob of fanatic Christians, led by Archbishop Theophilus" (Ency.Americanna).

The only reason for this destructive work was to conceal the fact that the "literature of the heathens" did not tell the same story that the pious biblical makers had put in their Bible.

And why does the Church still get so excited when some of that ancient literature is discovered? Because it fears the facts may be found.

Bible decoded

The facts have been found—and they are startling. They are related in books
by many able authors, and these books are burned by "fanatic Christians," or else
they are converted to the Light of Truth after reading these books.

Among other surprising things, these facts show that there was no early history
of the Hebrews as related in the Bible. And their reputed ancestors, Abraham, Isaac
and Jacob, are not historical figures, but mythical heros, analogous to those of
Homer and Hesiod.

Originally, these mythical heros were the gods that were associated with the
local sanctuaries in Palestine, and were adopted by the Hebrews when they settled in
that land.

The Pentateuchal narratives, the long discourses between God and the mythical
Moses, the Story of Creation, and many other events related in the Bible, are nothing
but fictitious compilations of the crafty priesthood for religious purposes, prepared
centuries after the Hebrews occupied Palestine, and are utterly worhtless as history.

Bible decoded.

CHAPTER VIII

Two Bodies In One

The multitude is lost in darkness. It looks for guidance to science and religion, and the leaders of science and religion are blindly wandering in the wilderness.

Orthodox religion in Christian countries igorantly follows and worships its Cruci
fied and Resurrected Jesus, who "washed us from our sins in his own blood" (Rev.1:5).
And if we just believe that he was the "only begotten Son," we shall "not perish,
but have everlasting life" (Jn.3:16).

That stupid philosophy removes Life from the realm of law and makes it subject
to man's belief. The church Fathers who invented that philosophy knew it was fraudulent. But it has been a great money-maker, and nothing else matters.

The realm of science is ruled by materialism. "The materialistic philosophy of

Bible decoded

the 19th century in which was reared the average modern scientist, has held its dogmatic power over his mind, altho matter itself has evaporated" (Arthur Koestler, the Sleepwalkers).

J. S. Haldane, the great astronomer, said, "Materialism, once a plausible theory, is now the fatalistic creed of thousands, but materialism is nothing better than a superstition, on the same level as a belief in withces and devils. The materialistic theory is bankrupt." (Bible Mysteries Revealed, Johan Wien).

That truly great scientist, Dr. Alexis Carrel, wrote, "The illusions of the mechanicists of the nineteenth century, the dogmas of Jacques Loeb, and the childish physico-chemical conceptions of the human being, in which so many physiologists, (biologists), and physicians still believe, have to be definitely abandoned" (Man The Unknown, p.108).

G. N. M. Tyrrell made this enlightening observation, "Now modern physics if beginning to discover the extending qualities of matter which entirely disrupt the theory that the material world is simple and self-contained. At the same time psychic research is discovering properties belonging to us which disrupt the same fallacy that we are self-contained within our bodies" (Light).

Carrel made a similar observation in these words: "Personality is rightly believed to extend outside the physical continuum. Its limits seem to be situated beyond the surface of the skin. The definiteness of the anatomical contours is partly an illusion. Man is certainly far larger and more diffuse than his body" (Man The Unknown, p.258).

If we shall ever effectuate some system that will present to the comprehension of the mind-conditioned masses the deeper problems of the Creative Cycle, we must flatly reject the absurd theory of science as to the nature of Life and the constitution of Man, and revive the Ancient Wisdom of the Wise Men of antiquity. We must rise above the plane of materialism and embrance the fact that the mysterious element called Life is not the produce of body function, BUT THE CAUSE OF IT.

Modern science teaches that body function produces Vitality, Mind, Consciousness and Intelligence, those strange qualities which make Man and which science can neither explain nor analyze.

Carrel declared that "our knowledge of the human body is, in truth, most rudimentary. It is impossible, for the present, to grasp its constitution. We must, then, be content with the scientific observation of our organic and mental activities, and, without any other guide, march forward into the unknown" (The Man Unknown, p.109).

This is a case of self-imposed ignorance that is preferable to the admission

that the Ancient Masters knew more about the Nature of Life and the constitution of Man than we do, and that they had solved most of the problems that are such a puzzle to modern science.

Much we want to know about Man and Life is told in a few words by the great

philosopher Paul, and appears in the 15th chapter of his Epistle to the Corinthians,

which is devoted to the Creative Cycle, but is badly garbled and distorted in the

Bible for the purpose of putting in the picture the mythical Jesus, a character whose

fraudulent history was not written until after Paul had been dead for more than two hundred and fifty years.

Paul declared, "The last enemy that shall be destroyed is Death" (vs.26).

How is Death going to be destroyed? That burning question is as old as the

race, but has never been scientifically explained by priest, nor preacher, nor science

If it were explained, the Church would fold up within a year, and medical art would soon be only a memory. But the great money-making schemes of this civilization are not that easily killed.

It is impossible to "destroy" any phase of a creative process, and that is what Death is. Death is a regular process of Creation and is ruled by the same law that governs Birth or any other process in the creative work. All we can do, and what we should do, is to remove, with proper understanding, the ignorance that surrounds Death with such horrific Fear.

Knowledge is based upon facts sets Man free from all Fear that rises from ignorance, darkness, deception, trickery, and false teaching (Jn.8:32). But as the Fear of Death is the very foundation of modern theology, all the power of the Mother Church would be used in the work of preventing the masses from being freed by proper knowledge from the Fear of Death.

The great philosopher Paul endeavored to remove the Fear of Death by citing the

Doctrine of the Ancient Masters, which he declared had been taught in all nations for

thousands of years, and long before the world ever heard of the gospel Jesus. That

Doctrine explained the Dual Nature of Man, showing that he is constituted of two

bodies instead of one, and Paul called these two bodies Celestial and Terrestrial

(1 Cor.15:40).

Harken to Paul: "We (must) continue grounded and settled in the faith (of the

Ancient Masters), and be not moved away from the hope of the gospel (of these Ancient Wise Men) which ye have heard (for a thousand years), and which was preached (by the Pagan Philosophers) to every creature which is under heaven, whereof I Paul am made a minister" (Col.1:23).

This very ancient gospel mentioned by Paul was definitely not the gospel of Jesus contained in the New Testament. It was the ancient Pagan Gospel that was taught in Asia Minor for two thousand years before the time of Paul, during the days of the worship of the Great Mother Cybele and her Virgin Born Son Atys, and was preached by the Ancient Astrologers ages before the mythical Jesus was invented by the Church Fathers to replace that ancient god Atys.

Paul mentioned the "raising of the dead," and said: "But some men will say, How are the dead raised up? and with what body do they come? Thou fool, that which thou sowest is not quickened, except it die. And that which thou sowest, thou sowest not that body which shall be, but bare grain" (vs. 35-37).

Then Paul proceeded to describe the two bodies of Man which appear as one to all those who live by sight, calling one of the bodies "celestial" and the other "terrestrial," and added:

"But the glory of the celestial is one (thing), and the glory of the terrestrial is another" (vs.40).

It is highly important to digress here and examine this mystery of two bodies, as a proper understanding of the Dual Bodies is the solution of the problem. We must comprehend the vast difference between the Celestial and the Terrestrial.

Gestation is the process of creation that occurs in the mother's womb, and this process is the work of the God Spirit as it builds the Terrestrial Body which will come into existence in the visible world in the process of birth.

Birth is the delivery of this created body from the womb. But the nature of this body thus born is not so readily determined. Science declares that it is nothing more than an organization of flesh, blood and bone. But the Ancient Masters taught that there is a Supreme, Intelligent Organizer that directs and performs this stupendous work, about which the greatest scientist of today knows so little, that he cannot imitate the simplest part of it. He cannot make a blade of grass nor a grain of corn, and knows so little about the body's constitution and function that he cannot make one drop of blood nor explain how the body makes it.

In its dumbness, science believes and declares that the body thus born is all there is to Man, and that the body was created in the mother's womb by the mother. If that were true, it would be one of the most astounding miracles in the universe. It is not true, but the belief that it is true is stubbornly asserted by science, and is taught in the schools and colleges.

Man is constituted of a dual nature, but science denies it. Paul definitely tells the world that Man has two bodies instead of one, and names them (1 Cor.15:40). And furthermore, the ancient Egyptian Book of The Dead presented a factual picture of this strange duality.

The Ancient Masters consistently taught that Man is constitued of two bodies, one the created body and the other the uncreated body, the one visible and the other invisible, the one temporal and the other eternal. The Egyptians called the uncreated unseen, invisible body the Ka. Paul called it the God Spirit that dwells in the Temple (body) (1 Cor.3:16). And science calls that ancient philosophy "heathenish superstition."

We shall never solve the mystery of Man by spurning and sneering the important point of Life and Man presented by the Ancient Masters. We have not yet made a single discovery concerning Life and Man that was not well-known to the Ancient Masters, and explained in the Ancient Scrolls in symbols and allegories which have been far beyond our understanding until quite recently.

Paul attempted to correct the error of living by sight, but only a few ever notice that. He said: "We look not at the things which are seen, but at the things which are not seen; for the things which are not seen are (created and) temporal; but the things which are not seen are (uncreated and) eternal" (2 Cor.4:18).

At another time he said: "For the invisible things of him from the Creation of the world are clearly seen (in the mind), being understood by the things which are made" (invisible) ... "Professing themselves to be wise, they become fools, and changed the glory of uncorruptible God (God Spirit dwelling in the body) into an image like

to corruptible (terrestrial, created) Man" (Romans 1:22,22,23).

That takes us clear back to the first chapter of Genesis, where the biblical

makers of the Mother Church interpolated in the Bible the statement that "God created

man in his own image" (Gen.1:27); and as a result of this fraudulent statements, the
artists have pictured God as a man with long hair and flowing whiskers.

And as Paul said, the glory of the uncorruptible God Spirit of the Universe has

been changed "into an image made like to corruptible man." And thus man makes his Gods.

The objects and images which are visible are the created forms, and they are

temporal, as Paul said. But the invisible Entities which are not seen with the eyes
are Uncreated and are Eternal.

In a further effort to explain the difference between the two bodies, the created and the uncreated, the visible and the invisible, Paul said:

"The first man is of the earth, earthy; the second man is the Lord from heaven.
As is the earthy, such are they (bodies) also that are earthy; and as is the heavenly
(Entities that animate the bodies), such are they also that are heavenly. And as we
have borne the image of the earthy, we shall also bear the image of the heavenly.
Now this I say, brethren, that flesh and blood (created body) cannot inherit the king-
dom of God; neither doth corruption inherit incorruption" (1 Cor.15:47-50).

"For we know that if our earthly house (created body) ... were dissolved, we
would have a building of God, an house not made with hands (Uncreated Entity), eternal
in the heavens" (2 Cor.5:1).

How could words make clearer the difference and distinction between the two
bodies? The "house not made with hands" is Paul's Second Man, the Celestial Man, the
uncorruptible God Spirit, the Uncreated Entity, and, by the ancient Egyptians was
called the Ka, and symbolized by them as a man-headed hawk (Budge, vol.2, p.299).

We suspect the statements in the Bible are not the exact words Paul used, as the
biblical makers always used their own terms and phrases in translating the ancient
scrolls, and this is admitted by the Mother Church in the Catholic Encyclopedia.

In Vol. IV, p.498, the Church states that it was the custom of the scribes
(biblical makers) to lengthen out here and there, to harmonize passages or to add
their own explanatory material. "Even the (Pauline) Epistles were greatly interpolated (corrupted and distorted) to lend weight to the personal views of their authors."

It is plain from the above quotations from the Bible, that Paul made a vast
differentiation between the two bodies. But modern science consistently scorns all
biblical statements, terming them as "heathenish rubbish," and the schools continue
teaching our children that Life, according to science, is just body function, and
when the body ceases to function, that is the end of Man and the extinction of Life,
the greatest element known.

We dislike the term God Spirit and don't believe Paul used those words. It was the tricky biblical makers of the Mother Church who, by their interpolation, distortion and corruption, created the fog where vision should be the clearest.

Spirit is fror the Latin Spiritus, and means to breathe. The Breath Man, the Breath World. Man became a Living Soul when God breathed into his nostrils the Breath of Life (Gen.2:7). Those thoughts and notions were invented by the biblical makers and were never copied from nor found in the Ancient Scrolls.

The Bible itself shows that the Ancient Masters regarded as Fire what we are taught to call God. Their God was Fire and they said so. And the Bible says "God is a consuming fire" (Heb.12:29, etc.). The first age of the earth was the Igneous Age says Prof. Hotema in his Cosmic Creation.

The first religion of which the modern world has any accurate account was that of Atlantis. This was the Fire Philosophy. It was an absolute philosophical ralition and gave to its votaries those powers which characterized one who has raised himself up to a plane above that of the earthly-minded.—Mysticism of Masonry by Dr. R.S.Clymer, p.180).

The Pythagoreans regarded what we call Fire as constituting the Heart of the Universe, the Monad or First Form, and postulated Fire as extending from the earth to the extreme limits of the Cosmos. They said that all things are derived from Fire, and strive ever to return to Fire. They proved their philosophy by showing that Fire transform every known substance to invisible gases. That further proves that every known substance and object can be nothing more than condensed gases.

Guy Atherton said: "The force of Fire disintegrates the binding elements of wood and releases the minerals and gases of which it is composed.

"We say the wood is burnt up. But we can see the ash that it left; and if the wood were burnt in a container that captures the gases, we can weigh them and find that no material has been lost.

"Indeed, no material has been fundamentally changed, either in the growing of the wood or in its burning....Each atom of carbon has retained its primary structure; each atom of the various gases of the air and of every other component has kept its individuality thruout both the growing of new wood as they were years before.

-47-

2 bodies in 1

"Jacques Loeb, the famous investigator, said that possibly the primal particles of Life are so infinitely small that they may travel on waves of light to other worlds' (Strange Powers, p.32).

However, as the Bible says Paul used the words God Spirit, we shall also to preserve the harmony. And it is the God Spirit, the Uncreated Entity, this Cosmic Spark of the Primordial Fire, operating in the womb of the mother, that clads itself in a material robe. But this robe is not created by the mother, nor built by her blood, as science teaches in the various schools and colleges, and as medical art believes.

In the Egyptian Book Of The Dead, written by scientific anthropolgists far ahead of modern science, there is a statement attributed to the God Spirit thus: "I am come into being (at birth) from matter. I have germinated (in the mother's womb) like things which germinate (in Mother Earth), and I have dressed myself like a tortoise."

In the case of Man, the God Spirit also dresses itself, and not with substance supplied by the mother's blood as modern science teaches. Creation builds New Bodies and these bodies are not made of old, second-hand material. Creation always uses new, fresh substance, and that substance comes not from the mother nor from her blood.

That new, fresh substance is composed of condensed Cosmic Rays, called Astral Light by the Ancient Masters, and discussed in detail by Prof. Hotema in his work titled "The Flame Divine."

Man comes forth at birth as the God of the Visible World, and is clad in a garment which corresponds with his earthly environment. This body was created by the God Spirit, working in the mother's womb, and the God Spirit can also dress itself "like a tortoise" when the occasion requires, using for the purpose new, fresh substance produced by the condensation of Cosmic Rays.

Back to the sowing of grain, Paul said that "it is sown in corruption; it is raised in incorruption.....It is sown a natural body; it is raised a spiritual body. There is a natural body and there is a spiritual body (1 Cor.15:42,44).

If Paul is literally quoted in the Bible at this important point, then he failed to inform his audience clearly as to the remarkable difference between what be called the natural body and the spiritual body.

2 bodies in 1

In this constantly changing world of illusion, where men are brain-washed and mind-conditioned from the cradle to the grave, they live in what they see and in what they are taught by the sordid institutions by which they are controlled, and they see not they think they see and fail to understand much that they do see and witness.

The reason why the Bible nowhere definitely teaches the plain facts of Creation and actually avoids the subject, is because the Church Fathers did not make their Bible for that purpose. They made it to serve the Church and not the people. They concealed the true facts of Creation and stressed the Fear of Death. For the Fear of Death is the leading factor that drives the mind-conditioned masses into the Church.

"Search the scriptures, for in them ye think ye have eternal Life" (Jn. 5:39). Remove the Fear of Death by a proper understanding of Death, by teaching the true facts of Creation, and the Church would quickly fade and vanish.

The natural body is the body we see. The spiritual body is the body we see not. The natural body is the terrestrial body; the spiritual body is the mysterious, unseen, uncreated, celestial body.

The Bible says, "Behold, the Kingdom of God is within you" (Luke 17:21). It is logical to assume that the King abides within his Kingdom. Hence, it is consistent to assume that God is within us, according to the Bible.

According to our views, Paul got mixed up in his attempt to explain some of the difference between the two bodies, provided he is literally quoted in the Bible. He said: "That was not first which is spiritual, but that which is natural; and afterward that which is spiritual....The first man (body) is of the earth, earthy; the second man (body) is the Lord from Heaven" (1 Cor.15:46,47).

Scientifically considered, this order should be reversed. The First Man is the God Spirit which dwells in the earthy Temple, the natural or terrestrial body, and, as we have just shown, that natural body is built up by the First Man or the God Spirit. And Paul said, "Know ye not that ye are the Temple of God, and that the Spirit of God dwelleth in you" (1 Cor. 3:16).

We must not fail to keep in mind the vast difference between these two bodies. One is the God Spirit, the Celestial Body, the Unseen, Uncreated, Real Man, the

-49-

Eternel Man, who has neither beginning nor ending, according to the Ancient Masters.

The natural body, the terrestrial body, the Temple of God, is the Created Body, and all created bodies have beginnings and endings.

But the uncreated elements of which the created bodies are constituted, and the Uncreated Entity, the God Spirit, which inhabits and dwells in these created bodies, is actually more eternal than the Sun itself. For the Sun is a created body, just as the human body is, and it is temporal, just as the human body is. But the elements of which the Sun is constituted are uncreated and are the eternal part which has neither beginning nor ending.

This is extra strong philosophy for brain-washed, mind-conditioned humanity. The student should now read the great works by Hotema titled (a) Pre-Existence of Man, (b) The Flame Divine, and (c) The Soul's Secret, and learn more of the details of this important phase of Life and Creation.

Grand Resurrection

CHAPTER IX

Ancient Terminology

The leading difficulty encountered in attempting to record and present the Ancient Wisdom, lies largely in the fact that the Mother Church had an army of priests and monks working for a thousand years in rewriting, revising and reshaping ancient history, in order to efface and obliterate all traces of the ancient terminology.

The scrolls from which the Church Fathers made their Bible had been written by the Ancient Astrologers, and dealt principally with the Science of the Astral Bodies and their effect and influence upon the earth and all things thereon. That was the very foundation of their philosophy and religion, a fact so generally known that no

Grand Resurrection

well-informed person of this age will contradict or deny it.

It was this very ancient asteristic philosophy to which Paul referred when he said he was a "minister of the gospel which was preached (by the Ancient Astrologers) to every creature which was under heaven" (Col.1:23).

Paul had been a student of that asteristic philosophy and was then a minister of it. The terminology of that philosophy was not the same as that used by the Church Fathers in making their Bible.

These Church Fathers quoted Paul as asserting that the human body is "the temple of God," and "the spirit of God dwelleth in you" (Cor.3:16). We shall grant that be used the word God, but in doing that he did not have in mind the Church God in the sky with long hair and flowing whiskers. He referred to the "Lord of the whole earth and that Lord was Man (Zech.4:14).

The ancients used "gods" to represent man and their conceptions of cosmic forces and cosmic phenomena. They employed them as symbols of what they thought they should be as religionists.

Their gods were symbolic, allegoric, parabolic, emblematic devices of the imagination, and signified nothing but their ideal, imaginary objects and elements which were put into them by the people for the people; and these gods do nothing except what the people perform thru them in their names for themselves. Man makes gods and does everything for them. The gods do nothing for him.

Ancient terminology

The "Spirit of God" and the "God Spirit" are terms that were never used by and were unknown to the Ancient Astrologers. The terms "spirit," "spiritual," "spiritualism," "spiritual world," and "spiritual man" were invented by the Church Fathers for the purpose of concealing and obliterating the asteristic terminology of the Ancient Astrologers, whose philosophy they filched, revised, revamped and presented as Christianity.

Having thus disposed of the terminology of the Ancient Astrologers by replacing it with a new one, it is exceedingly difficult to penetrate the wall erected by this new terminology around the brain-washed, mind-conditioned masses in the "Spiritual

Ancient terminology

World" of Christianity.

Having been born, reared and educated for a thousand years in the "Spiritual World" of Christianity, the masses in that world are lost and confused when their Christian terminology is taken from then and the asteristic terminology of the Ancient Astrologers is presented.

We must get our feet back on solid ground and learn the facts, or stay right where we are put. There is an astral world but no spiritual world. There is an astral man but no spiritual man. There is an astral God but no Spiritual God. There is an astral force but no spiritual force.

And as we have used the Christian terminology in our discussion of Paul's Epistle as to the dual bodies of man in order to preserve the harmony for the benefit of those students who know nothing of the true terminology of the Ancient Wisdom, we shall now change and replace that false, empty, worthless "spiritualism" of Christianity with the sound, basic Asterialism of the Ancient Astrologers.

Creation

The popular theory of Creation, based on the teachings of theology, is to the effect that something comes from nothing. For instance, the Church God, who can do everything with nothing, just said, "Let there be light; and there was light" (Gen. 1:3).

The whole biblical story of Creation in Genesis makes a good fairy tale for children, and that is the exact attitude of the Church toward the masses. When children have outgrown their Santa Claus and rise to a higher level, they are given Jesus and go right on with their fairies.

In his "Pre-Existence of Man" Prof. Hotema teaches that there can be no actual existence without potential existence. There could be no actual water if there were no potential water in the form of invisible vapor. Something comes not from nothing; and the something which comes, must describe with exact precision the something from which it comes.

Like begets like is the universal law without a single exception.

The begotten and the begetter must be of the same nature. The begotten must describe with exact precision the qualities of the begetter.

Ancient terminology

According to the law, life comes only from life, corn only from corn, man only from man, and god only from god. Apples never come from oranges and wheat never comes from oats. If there are gods in heaven, there must be gods on the earth.

That is what the Ancient Masters taught. They regarded Man as a God, and called the Lord of the whole earth (Zech.4:14). He had dominion over everything upon the earth (Gen.1:28). The student here should read what Prof. Hotema said about Man in his Cosmic Creation.--

"Man is the highest known organized entity in the Universe, the Supreme Being of the various kingdoms of the earth." Under the law, Man could not be that on the earth plane if he were not that on the heavenly plane.

Study the Interlaced Triangles of the Ancient Masters. In that symbol the earthy Man below is the image and the likeness of the heavenly Man above. But had the Ancient Masters taught what the Church teaches, this symbol would have presented God above and Man below.

Such a god the Ancient Masters did not have. Such a god is found nowhere in their symbols nor in their philosophy. Where such a god appears in the ancient scriptures, it is the fraudulent work of the Church Fathers who revised and reshaped those scriptures.

Paul taught the ancient philosophy and said so. He declared: "As if the earthy, such are they also that are earthy; and as is the heavenly, such are they also that are heavenly. And as we have borne the image of the earthy, we shall also bear the image of the heavenly" (1 Cor.15:48,49).

That declaration is clear and plain and agrees perfectly with the symbolism of the Interlaced Triangles. By a process of transformation, not of creation, Man in the heavenly world appears as Man in the earthy world, and he returns to the heavenly world by the same process of transformation in reverse, which we call Death, or Born Again (John 3:3,5,7).

It is the Man in the earthy world that confuses and deceives all them that live by sight and look at the things which are seen, as Paul said. They regard as Man the body they see, which is erroneous, but which agrees with the teachings of the scientist the materialist, the religionist and the evolutionist. This is one of the big errors that Paul tried to correct, as we have explained under "Two Bodies in One."

Ancient Terminology

The requirements of reason dictate and the logic of science necessitates the direct conclusion that:—

1. Every effect indicates the existence of a cause.
2. The cause must be anterior to the effect.
3. The cause must also be interior to the effect, as the facts of evolution signify.
4. The cause is an Invisible Principle evolving to effects.
5. The cause must be the efficient and sufficient equal of the effects.
6. The cause must answer to all the requirements of all the effects.
7. Conscious Being must rise from Cosmic Being that is described in Conscious Being.

Creation of Men

The Bible says that man was created by a God, but the findings of science do not support that claim.

Col. James Churchward, author and traveler, wrote: "Under the great Law of Creation, there must first come a CONDITION, and, with it (there comes) a suitable life (living forms) to live in it.....The Condition (of the Cosmos) is the Parent of the Creation.

"Thruout the entire history of the earth this has been so; and at no time do we find the new Creation behind the Condition, because the Condition is the Parent of the Creation."--Lost Continent of Mu, p.328.

The Ancient Astrologers knew, and Deductive Science shows, that no living thing can come into existence until the condition of the environment is such as to DRAW POTENTIAL EXISTENCE INTO ACTUAL EXISTENCE ON THE VISIBLE PLANE.

Confused are they who live by sight, because they regard this event as a case of Creation, which means to the Inductive Scientist, the Evolutionist, the theologist, and the unprepared mind the coming of something from nothing.

That never occurs. There is a Cause for every Effect. Causes are invisible forces, while effects are visible products.

What is usually termed Creation is the Transformation of invisible potentiality to visible actuality, as the transformation of vapor to water. That illustrates what is commonly called and believed to be Creation.

The Ancient Astrologers taught that the visible world is a condensed objective of the vast invisible realm, in which there must exist all things that appear in the visible world.

Ancient Terminology

This is the ancient Doctrine of Pre-Existence, which Prof. Hotema has discussed in his work of that title, which shows that Potential Being dwells in the Aeriferous Substance which surrounds the earth and contains, as the Ancient Astrologers taught, the Archeus or Astral Beginning of all Cosmic Phenomena, called Nature.

This ancient doctrine is briefly mentioned in the Bible in these words: "These are the generations of the heavens and of the earth when they were created, in the day that God made the earth and the heavens, and every plant of the field before it was in the earth, and every herb of the field before it grew" in the earth (Gen.2:4,5).

When the condition of the earth is favorable for living things to appear, that condition activates the Creative Principle, causing Potential Existence to evolve, unfold, and appear as Actual Existence, clothed in a garment that harmonizes with the Cosmos, corresponding in color, number and vibration to the Solar System as it was at the time when the transformation occurred,--when the building of God, an house not made with hands, eternal in the heavens, appears, as if by magic, as Visible Man in the visible world (2 Cor.5:1).

We are not certain whether Churchward knew what he wanted to say and meant just what he said. To be more specific and exact, the Condition of the Environment or earth is not the Parent of Creation. It is the Universal Activator of the Creative Principle. And no living thing comes into actual existence until the Condition of the Environment is such as to activate the Creative Principle and draw that particular Entity of the invisible world from Potential Existence into Actual Existence.

The earth would still be populated with Dinosaurs and Mastodons had the Condition of the Earth remained suitable for their existence. So we may say the Condition of the Earth also governs the Kind of living forms that appear in the visible world. It was a change in the Condition of the Earth that caused those giant animals to perish and vanish.

Man remains and goes on and on because he possesses greater ability to adjust himself to the changing conditions of his environment.

Prof. Hotema says in his Cosmic Creation that the experience of millions of years has shown, that when the earth became the home of visible man, it became the partner of a being that is not only the King of Life and the Climax of Creation upon the earth but he is as eternal as the elements of which the earth and the sun are composed.

Ancient Terminology

The evidence of millions of years shows that man not only goes on while the other races of animals perish and vanish, but he will still continue after the earth itself will have exploded and disintegrated into the dust of which it was originally made.

For countless ages man gloated over the dark waters of the primitive sea, looking and waiting for a suitable spot to materialize so that he could step out on the new-born earth, says Hotema in Cosmic Creation (p.119).

Glorious
Resurrection

CHAPTER X

Mystic Sleep

One of the ancient fables dealing with the Birth of Man was the Mystic Sleep, mentioned by Prof. Hotema in his Pre-Existence of Man, and on which the Church Father based their fraudulent story in the 11th chapter of the John Gospel relative to the "Raising of Lazarus."

It is shocking to see what the Church Fathers did in compiling their Bible from the Ancient Scrolls. The more we discover the more we see that the Bible is the most fraudulent book that was ever published. It is called the Inspired Word of God. We could not safely put any faith in that kind of a God. The MADE if like the MAKER. No faith can be put in the Church nor in anything the Church has made.

The Ancient Masters fabulized the Birth of Man in the Terrestrial World as the Death and Burial of the Ego in a physical prison. They symbolized this event in Card 12 of the Tarot as a man hanging by one foot, his head down, and arms tied behind his back. This is the meaning of the Black Pentacle.

The various commentators missed the point in their interpretation of the symbolism of this card. Some titled the card Prudence; others called it Judgment. Dr. Waite termed it one "of profound significance," but, said he, all the significance is veiled, and continued:

"It has been falsely called a card of Martyrdom, a card of Prudence, a card of the Great Work, a card of Duty. But we may exhaust all published interpretations and find only vanity." Then he added:

"I'll say simply on my own part that the card expresses the relation, in one of its aspects, between the Divine and the Universe. He who can understand that the story of his higher nature is imbedded in this symbolism, will receive intimations concerning the great awakening that is possible, and will know that after the Sacred Mystery

Glorious
Resurrection

of Death, there is a Glorious Mystery of Resurrection" (Key To The Tarot).

Waite's assertions indicate that he knew more than he said. And he was the only
one of the many commentators on the Tarot who have dome to our notice, who appeared

to sense there is a certain connection between Death and Resurrection not for just the
gospel Jesus, but for all mankind.

The Ancient Masters designed Tarot Card 12 to symbolize the Birth of Man in the
Terrestrial World. They taught that in Birth, "the Ego becomes 'cribbed, cabined,

and confined' in the narrow limits of the earthy body, and lost at each step on the
descending path (to birth), a dimension of Consciousness. The Ego becomes bound at

Birth in the sensual and palpable, after previously having had the glorious liberty
to range at will (like a Radar Beam) thru limitless space and universal thought."

Mystic sleep

According to the Wise Men of the Ancient World, when Astral Man creates a body
and confines himself in it so he may appear on the physical plane, he suffers a serious diminution of Consciousness, termed a swoon. This state continues as long as the

Ego dwells in the earthy body, or during the earthly existence of Man.

From this philosophy there developed the fable of the Mystic Sleep. This referred to Solar Man during his days of confinement in the created body. According
to the Bible, he was regarded as "dead," yet "was also considered to be alive." (Rev.
3:1).

Mention is made in the Bible of the Solar Spark, the Clear Flame, shining bright-
ly in the Celestial World, but sinking "into deep mire" upon Incarnation, or when the
Solar Spark, in the mother's womb, is being merged in the developing physical organism.

The Bible says: "The waters are come into my soul. I sink in deep mire, where
there is no standing. I am come into deep waters, where the floods overwhelm me"
(Ps.69:1,2).

Right there in the Bible is the ancient allegory relating to the Solar Spark,
in the mother's womb, being merged in the damp physical organism. And the Birth of
Man is symbolized in the Tarot as the "Hanged Man." This state was signified in the
Ancient Mysteries by the Black Pentacle.

Water, not in its fluidistic form, was the primary aspect of substance in the
oldest mythologies and cosmologies, which the Church Fathers called "pagan rubbish."

Water was the primal substance of the Universal Mother. Basically, Mother,
Matter and Water were considered as one by the Ancient Masters. Plato mentioned
Water as "the liquid of the whole vivification."

Card 17 of the Tarot presents a nude female who has one foot upon the land and
one foot upon a pool of water, signifying the dual nature of Man.

Mystic sleep

The female is Hathor, or Mother Nature, and the most dual sign of the Zodiac is Gemini. This sign, pictured among the Constellation as the Twins, symbolized the Celestial and Terrestrial Bodies of Man, mentioned in the Bible (1 Cor.15:40).

The female pours fluid from a silver cup into the pool, to indicate the positive pole of Polarity; and she pours fluid from a golden cup upon the land to denote the negative pole of Polarity, thus indicating the male and female qualities of humanity.

In ancient mythology, the Living Fire must dry out a path across the Sea of Generation, so Celestial Man may cross the reed (Red) Sea out of Egypt, signifying the created body, and enter the Bright Land of the Celestial World, which is never darkened by the shadow of the Black Pentacle, the Created Body.

At the end of a shower, an eloquent symbol, the Rainbow, appears in view to edify the mind of him who can think. In its sevenfold coloration we see again the septenary design of Cosmic Creation, including Man.

The one cosmic essence of clear light, shining thru falling water, is naturally subdivided into Seven Constituent Rays, revealing the Seven-Rayed Formation of Man.

All created forms are septenary in structure. Every cycle runs its natural course and comes to perfection in seven subcycles. The constant reminder of this to him who knows, is the Rainbow which appears at the end of a shower.

And so, Man, at the end of his sojourn in the watery habitat of the created body, will have completed his perfection in seven stages, and will then need no more immersions in the Sea of Generation.

The seven stages are variously symbolized in the Bible. They appear as "the seven heads (which) are seven mountains," and also as the Seven Kings (Rev.17:10).

In his initiation in the Egyptian Mysteries, the Neophyte was made acquainted with the fable of the Mystic Sleep and the secret of the Glorious Resurrection.

He was also shown a dummy figure of Ausares (Osiris, Lazarus) on its funeral bier, at the head of which stood Neophythys, and at the foot, Isis, falsely presented in the Bible as the "two sisters of Lazarus" who weep for him.

O you Pious Church Fathers, how skillfully you could falsify. You were Past Masters at the trick. Your equal never lived, and your slaves never die.

Hovering over the body of Ausares was "a hawk with outstretched wings" (Rudge), which symbolized the Ego leaving the created body at death. This scene was to teach the Neophyte how Celestial Man looks down on his created body after he leaves it at death.

Events are constantly occurring now which simulate this fictitious scene presented to the Neophyte in the Ancient Mysteries five thousand years ago. Accounts of these appear in various publications, and Prof. Hotema mentioned a case in his

"Cosmic Creation," 2nd. edition.

A similar account appeared in Fate Magazine for March, 1960, titled "My Proof Of Survival", in which a certain man described his drowning and his rescue from the waters of the ocean. He said:

Mystic sleep

"From my present perspective of more than twenty years, I look back with awe upon the moment in July, 1929, when I drowned." He continued:

I was in the ocean and "suddenly a mountainous wave broke over me. I went down, down, down, into the quiet depths of the dark waters. . . . .I felt peace settle over me. . .It seems then that a wonderful transition suddenly occurred. I was no longer in the water, but high above it, looking down upon it.

"The sky, which had been grey and lowering, was now irridescent with indescrible beauty. There was music that I seemed to feel rather than to hear. Waves of ecstatic and delicate color vibrated around me, and lulled me to a sense of peace beyond earthly comprehension.

"On the water beneath me a boat came into view, with two men. . .in it. Then saw a blob of something floating in the water. A wave tossed it and rolled it over. And there I was looking into my own distorted face. What a relief, I thought, that I need that ungainly body no longer.

"Then I saw the men lift the body into the boat, and my vision vanished. The next thing I knew, it was dark and I was lying on the beach, cold and sick and sore. Men were working over me, and I was later told that they worked over me for more than two hours to revive me.

"I find myself wondering, even now, what would have happened had those life guards come just a little later."

These strange events, occurring constantly all over the world, show that there is a Future Life, and confirm the teachings of the Ancient Masters. But that is insufficient to persuade modern science to change its opinion of Life and Death. According to science, when body function ceases, that is the end of Man and the termination of Life.

The Great Resurrection
By Prof. Hilton Hotema
Available in Aug.1960.

CHAPTER XI

The Life Cycle

There can be no action in the entire Universe without reaction, and in Expiration without Resurrection.

Solar Man could not exist after the demise of the body if he did not exist before the body were created.

"Matter, the slave of Man, is (indestructible and) immortal. Could anything be more preposterous than to assume that this Master dies at the grave, and the slave lives on forever? John Bigelow, in After Days.

"There is no death. Man has one life on two worlds. When he leaves the physical body he simply changes to another life under new conditions while remaining in essence the same as he was on the earth" (Huntley, in Harmonics of Evolution, p.70).

"We shall not sleep (in death), but we shall all be changed (to immortality)... As we have borne the image of the earthy, we shall also bear the image of the heavenly. And death is swallowed up in victory. O Death, where is thy sting? O Grave, where is thy victory?"—The Bible, 1 Cor.15.

"There is no Birth without Death, and no Death without Birth. Man lives to die and dies to live. No state of existence can begin unless a previous one ends. There is no process in the entire Universe that is not dependent for its continuity upon Cyclic Change; and as surely as Day follows Night, so must Life follow Death" (Dr. James Clark, In Eternal Time.)

We know that Life is a real agency, yes, by far the most potent factor in the development of the seed. Neither the earthly elements nor the physical forces used to clothe and form the seed, have any power of their own to assume the shape of the seed and exercise its function. It has inherent endowments of immense potentialities. In a word, the seed's Life is the great fact of the phenomena of its being rather than its form or the constitutients of its body. And the mind is not satisfied with the facile explanation that the cosmos carefully preserves the packing case but throws away the Treasure it contained.

Then, whence has the Life of the seed gone? Is all Life one vital force, and has the seed-life merely returned to the great stream from which it may have come?

That would be a simple explanation, and it is the accepted one for many minds. But Sir Oliver Lodge expressed the view of the modern esoteric when he said, "The Ego may return to the central store, but not without identity."

Dr. Robert Walter stated, "Whatever may be said of Life in its lower manifestations, we think no one will doubt that in its human form it never loses its individuality by being returned to the source whence it came.

Life Cycle

"The immortality of Life is proved in the same way as the indestructibility of matter. . . .The human being surely becomes individualized once for all, and having

learned much from earthly experience, he returns to the source from whence he came, to carry with him thru all the future whatever he may have gained. It is not to be

presumed that his opportunities for gain will ever cease, and all men necessarily carry with them the products of the past" (Vital Science, p.178).

According to the Ancient Masters, the incarceration of the Ego in the Terrestrial Cross (Human Body) is the creative process that forms and fixes as an eternal Entity the Individual Consciousness of man on the Astral Plane.

That is the purpose of earthly Life. That is the reason why Solar Man comes in-- to existence in an earthy body on the earthy plane. That is the Cosmic Process by which Individuality emerges from Universality.

The Masters taught that Seven Incarnations are required in general to accomplish that definite state of Eternal, Individual Consciousness. They held that the Law of Seven ruled in the realm of Life just as it did in other fields of Creation.

Seven is the number of incarnations recorded in the Apocalypse, together with the Seven Sense Powers and the Seven Great Nerve Centers of the body, making Revelation the Book of Sevens.

The Bible tells the story in these words: "There are seven kings (incarnations) and five (incarnations) are fallen (have come to pass), and one (more incarnation) is, and the other (incarnation) is not yet come" (Rev. 17:10).

The original scribe of Revelation, who was none other than the great philosopher Apollonius of Tyaneus (born February 16, A.D.2), referred to the Seven Incarnations, calling them kings, as we have observed.

Volumes have been written about the dual constitution of man, and the Bible teaches that Man is a denizen of two worlds, calling them the celestial and the terrestrial. We would call them astral and physical, invisible and visible.

And volumes have been written about the dual constitution of man, and the Bible teaches that he is a dual being, constituted of two bodies, which are called the celestial and the terrestrial (1 Cor.15:40).

The puzzle appears in the name given in the Bible to the Celestial body. The mind-conditioned masses immediately think of a God in the sky when the Celestial Body is called the God Spirit. Paul said, "Know ye not that ye (the body) are the temple (of the Spirit) of God, and that the Spirit of God dwelleth in you" (1 Cor. 3:16).

We have learned so much about the way the Church Fathers twisted and distorted the biblical passages to realize that Paul did not make the statements attributed here to him. But enough was said to show that Paul taught the duality of Man and identified the dual bodies.

In The Soul's Secret Prof. Hotema said:

1. Man is constituted of dual bodies.

Life cycle

2. Demonstration has shown that the physical and astral bodies may temporarily separate without causing physical death, and this secret was taught the Neophtye in the Ancient Mysteries.

3. During such separation, the intelligent Ego is still attached to the physical body by a radiatory beam called in the Bible the Silver Cord (Eccl.12:6), as explained by Hotema in The Flame Divine.

4. It is the intelligent Ego that engineers and effects this release.

5. By personal contact and acquaintence with ex-human beings, the student discovers that man lives on indefinitely as the Ego, while his discarded body disintegrates and returns to the gases of the Astral Plane.

6. The student thus proves that man is an astral being, destined to live eternally in the astral form. He thus discovers that man's physical body confines the astral Entity, or that earthy man is the Ego clad in a garment that corresponds with his environment.

7. The discovery of the nature of man is true of all living animals. Each is modled upon a superior and eternal Ego.

The God Spirit that dwells in the human temple is none other than the Real Self. For man has within himself all the potentalities of his own being. No god but himself dwells in his body.

The Real Self, while dwelling in the body, is the Crucified God, and the Real Self is the Resurrected God when the cosmic process called Death liberates the Real Self from the body.

The Real Self, not a mythical god in the sky, built the body in the mother's womb, and, in so doing, the Real Self confined and crucified itself in the body, which the Ancient Masters called the Prison of the Ego.

They taught that the Real Self, called the God Spirit in the Bible, is as dead as it can ever be while confined in the body. That was the Crucified God myth. And they taught that the Real Self, the God Spirit, is liberated from the prison in death. That was the Resurrected God myth.

And so, the last enemy that shall be destroyed is Death. For Death is swallowed up in victory. O Death, where is thy sting? O Grave, where is thy victory?--1 Cor. 15:26,54,55.

Since it is a fact that the Ego is the Eternal Entity, then our natural existence is not that in the flesh, but that which we live outside of the body which we inhabit on the earthy plane. And the ancient Egyptians who had developed a religion in which life on the earthy plane was merely a preperation for the natural existence in the celestial world, shows that they wer wise in a measure far beyond us.

Death is as natural as birth. It is an orderly separation of the dual parts which constitute Man in the changing world of illusion. Death is the regular cosmic process of the Glorious Resurrection, called Born Again in the Bible (Jn.3:3,5,7).

In the very ancient Egyptian Book Of The Dead, Death is regarded as the Resurrection of the Ka-image of Man, the Incorrupt, Immortal Being. It is the "coming

Life cycle

forth (from the dark body) to the glorious Light, to the higher Life attainable in the
heaven of Eternity." The Ego is mentioned as "projecting itself into one physical
embodiment after another, steppeth onward thru eternity."

In the death process, the Uncreated Man leaves behind the corruptible, terrestric
body, and he returns to the Celestial World of Glory, called Heaven by Christianity,
but without knowing what the term means or how we get there.

The event termed Death was indicated by the Egyptians in a symbolic form, which
showed Osiris (Created Man) lying on a bier, and the Uncreated Man (Ka-image), leaving the body as a flying hawk (Budge).

After Uncreated Man leaves the Created Body, the latter goes thru a slow process
of dissolution, as mentioned by Paul (2 Cor. 5:1), in which the Created Body returns
to the original elements of which is was composed, and these elements, as cosmic
gases, follow Celestial Man back to the Celestial World, the original source from
whence they came.

The process of Death is that mysterious "change" to which Paul referred in these
words:--

"Behold, I show you a mystery: We shall not sleep (in death), but we shall all

be changed (to Immortality) in a moment, in the twinkling of an eye, at the last

trump; for the trumpet (of Gabriel) shall sound, and the dead (the Ego that dies not)

shall be raised incorruptible, and we shall be changed" (by passing from Terrestrial
to Celestial existence) (1 Cor. 15:51,52).

There it all is, right in the Bible. In the Egyptian Book of The Dead, the
transition to Asterism, called Spiritualism by Christianity, is thus described,

"This thou doest in one little moment of time."

In elucidating the Tibetan Book Of The Dead, Evans-Wentz said: "In a moment of
time, perfect enlightenment is obtained" (p.168).

The mysterious process of leaving the created body in death has been described
by one who made an unexpected recovery from a long, death-like swoon, and who said

that it is like struggling thru a dark, narrow tunnel into a big, brilliantly illumi-
nated space.

He said that in the Dying Process, the Mind grows clearer than ever before in

earthly life; the head, mentioned in the Bible as the Golden Bowl (Eccl.12:6), actu-

ally becomes intensely brilliant like glittering gold; and the Silver Cord, also

mentioned in the Bible (Eccl.12:6), and which consists of an invisible beam of Astral

Radiation that materializes into the Spinal Cord that actually links Earthy Man with
Astral Man, grows stronger to protect the Immortal Ego. And "the etheric body," says

another author, "flows out of the body (thru the Fonticulus Frontalis in the top of

-63-

Life cycle

the head) like a rapidly moving flurescent light, imperceptibly extracting the body's vitality, somewhat like a suction pump," and the Immortal Ego, the Celestial Body mentioned by Paul, leaves the Terrestrial Body thru the top of the head, the "door opened in heaven" (Rev.4:1), as Asterial Light that may be seen by a true clairvoyant.

CHAPTER XII

Swindle Of Mythography

Keeping man in darkness and receiving him is the profitable scheme that seems to have no limit. It begins everywhere and extends everywhere.

It fools the unwary with such attractive terms as the Secret Doctrine, the Sacred Magic, Occult Knowledge, the Key which unlocks the Mystery of Divine Creation, so a

common person may learn it, use it, and thus Command the Hidden Forces of Nature.

The Church Fathers, in the making of their Book They Blamed On God, were experts in the art of deception. They could get more out of one WORD than modern science can get out of an atomic bomb.

They said, The Word was in the begin ing, and the Word was with God, and the Word was God (John 1:1). It would be hard to beat that one.

The Masons picked this up and they have their mysterious Lost Word, said to be a Word of surpassing value, and claiming a profound veneration.

This mysterious Word at length was lost, they assert, and a temporary substitute for it was adopted.

The Jews had a Word too sacred to be pronounced, and it was always spelt. Because they were forbidden to pronounce it, they called it the Ineffable Name.

And all this forbidding was for the purpose of deceiving the "man of darkness" and concealing the fact that the sacred Ineffable Name applied not to any god, but to the Sacred Four Elements of Creation.

The four letters of the Ineffable Name were J H V H, pronounced Yod He Vau He, and termed the Tetragrammation. It referred to no god, but to the symbolical tetrad, represented in the Ancient Mysteries by the Four Forms of the ancient Sphinx, —Man, Eagle, Lion and Bull.

These were the four fixed Zodiac Signs, and they, with all their analogies, ex-

-65-

plained that one mysterious Word hidden in all the sanctuaries of the ancient world,
and this Word, according to the scribe of the John gospel, was God.

The Sacred Four

The Sphinx, found in all lands of the ancient world, was designed to symbolize
the Sacred Four Elements, Fire, Air, Water, Earth.

The finding of the Four Elements in objects and phenomena of quite different
categories, between which the "man of darkness" sees nothing in common, the Initiate
sees the analogy between all objects and all phenomena, and is convinced that all ob-

jects are constructed and constituted according to the same law and the same plan.

The conception is quite clear: If the Ineffable Name (Four Elements) is in everything, then everything should be analogous to the whole,--the atom analogous to the
Universe, and all analogous to the Ineffable Name. And a study of the Ineffable Name

and the finding it in everything, constituted the chief goal of Kaballistic philosophy.

The Four Archangels, Michael, Gabriel, Raphael and Phannel, are only another
vestment for the Four Elements. Clement of Alexandria wrote:

"These Four Powerful Ones, these Four Canobs, these Heavenly Architects, emanate
from the Supreme Infinite One (Cosmic Gas), and evolve the Universe from Chaos" (Sacred Symbols of Mu, by Churchward, p.79).

And so, according to the Bible, we have pin-pointed God. The Word was God, and
God was the Word, and the Word represented and related to the Sacred Four Elements,
symbolized in the ancient world as "The Great Builders of the Universe."

Then, there is the Masonic story "of the assassination, the burial, the finding,
and the raising of Hiram Abiff," says a work titled Doctrine Of Kabalism," which
continues:

This event "is made clear by comparing it with the pictured symbols of this
Arcanum," referring to Card 3 of the Ancient Tarot. "It thus, in reality, is the key

to the Master's word which lost at that time.

"The G of Masonry, found traced upon the breast of the murdered Hiram, is the
letter of this Arcanum (the Hebrew letter Gimel, which means to warm, to cherish, and
to ripen). High twelve, the time the Master was attacked, is represented by the

noon-day position of the Sun. Low twelve, the time he was buried, is indicated by the
position of the moon at the nadir.

"The grave (of Hiram), which is six feet deep due east and west, and six feet
perpendicular, is represented by the six-sided cube upon which Isis sits (in Tarot
Card 3). The sprig of acassia marking the grave is presented in the Tarot as a phallic

scepter. The twelve Masons sent out to hunt for Hiram are symbolized by the twelve
stars above the head of Isis. The five points of fellowship upon which Hiram was
raised (from the dead) by means of the grip of the Lion's paw, are indicated by the
five eyes traced upon the cube (upon which Isis sits); and the final transcendent
result of so being raised (from the dead) is pictured by the eagle on the left hand
of Isis" (p.114).

If we ask a Master Mason what lessons he learned from this ritual, he will say
not much that made sense. If we ask a dozen more the same question, we will get
similar answers. Even the instructors, the Master of Ceremonies, do not have the
answer that accords with the philosophy of the Ancient Masters.

Tarot Card 3, The Empress

We shall proceed to notice the symbolism of this Card and interpret it to show
what the Neophyte was taught about Creation when he was initiated in the Ancient
Mysteries, the parent of modern Masonry.

This card presents a woman, with two great wings, which are absent in some pictures. She sits upon the Throne of the Sun, with Five Eyes inscribed on the front
side of it. In her right hand is an escutcheon bearing an Eagle with outstretched

wings, and in her left hand she holds a Scepter surmounted by a globe and the symbol
of Venus. She is adorned with a crown of Twelve Stars, and has a Lunar Crescent under
her feet. In front of her, in some pictures, a field of grain is maturing.

The Empress is mentioned in the Bible as follows: "And there appeared a great
wonder in heaven; a woman clothed with the Sun, and the Moon under her feet, and upon her head a Crown of Twelve Stars" (Rev.12:1).

The Empress symbolizes Nature. She signifies growth, development, product, and
indicates the work of the Sacred Four Elements.

Being "clothed with the Sun" implies universal fecundity. The Eagle signifies
the Immortal Ego of Man. The Moon under her feet indicates the fuction of generation.
The Scepter, crowned by the symbol of Venus, reprecents the high office of Motherhood.

Her diadem, with Twelve Stars, shows that the Empress personifies the principles
and powers of the Macrocosm which produces the governs the Microcosm, as symbolized
by the Twelve Signs of the Sodiakos.

The combined qualities of the Empress signify the Cycle Of Life. She represents
the Gate of Entrance into the created world, as into the Garden of Venue.

To complete the Life Cycle, she holds the Eagle, which represents the Immortal
Ego which knows the secret of the mysterious path that extends out into the vast
realm of the invisible world,--which is the theme of Card 20, The Resurrection.

And now we shall notice the emptiness of the Masonic ritualism as compared with
that of the Ancient Mysteries, its parent.

One of the principal purposes of initiation was to teach the Neophyte, who had

Glorious
Resurrection

been prepared, tested, and accepted, and who is symbolized in the Bible as a Lamb facing "sacrifice" (Revl5:6), that Golden Secret of the Ancient Masters concerning the mysterious Astral World, lying just over the hill which all living things must travel, and about which Masonry teaching little worth while.

P.D. Ouspensky presents his interpretation of the symbolism of this Tarot Card as follows:

"I felt the breath of spring; and the fragrance of violets, lilies of the valley and the soft singing of elves was borne toward me. Brooks murmured, green tree-tops rustled, innumerable choirs of birds were singing, bees were droning, and everywhere was the joyful living of Nature.

"The Sun shone softly and mildly, a small white cloud hung over the forest. In the midst of a green glade where bloomed the first yellow primroses, on a throne encircled with ivy and blossoming lilac, I saw the Empress.

"A green wreath adorned her golden hair. Twelve Stars shone above her head. Two snow-white wings were visible behind her back, and in one hand she held a Scepter.

"With a tender smile the Empress looked about her, and beneath her glance flowers opened and buds unfolded their green leaves. The whole of her dress was covered with flowers, as though every flower that opened was reflected or imprinted on it and became a part of her garment.

"The sign of Venus, the Goddess of Love, was carved upon her marble throne.

"'Oh, Queen of Life' I said, 'why is everything so radiant and joyful and happy around you? Do you not know that there is the grey, weary autumn, the cold, white winter? Do you not know that there is death, black graves, cold damp sepulchres, cemeteries?

"'How can you smile so joyfully looking at the unfolding flowers, when all dies and all will die, when all is condemned to death--even that which is not yet born?"

"The Empress looked at me smiling, and beneath her smile I suddenly felt that in my soul the flower of some bright understanding was opening, as though something was being revealed to me, and I felt the terror of death beginning to depart from me."

Tarot Card 12, The Hanged Man

The symbolism of this card presents the philosophy of the Ancient Masters concerning the Birth of Man on the earthy plane. In the picture appears a man, with his hands tied behind his back, hanging by one leg from a high gallows, with his head

downward, around which was a Golden Halo. Here we quote Ouspensky:

"New suffering, such as no earthly misfortune can ever cause, that is what awaits man on the earth when he finds the path to Eternity and the understanding of the Infinite.

"He is still a man, but he already knows many things inaccessable even to gods. And this conflict between the big and the little in his soul makes his torture on his Golgotha.

"In his own soul a high gallows is raised on which he hangs in suffering, feeling as though he was turned head downward.

"It is for this that he went on a long journey from trial to trial, from initiation, thru failures and thru falls."

The Prodigal Son

The story of Man on earth is depicted in the Bible as the prodigal son who left his Father's house (the Celestial as Paul called it in 1 Cor. 15:40), and goes to a far country, which is this earth, or the terrestrial.

Man's whole life experience on this earthly, terrestrial plane, is "the far country."

Birth is Crucifixion. The Ego is crucified by Birth in the body which forms the Cross when man stands erect with feet together and arms extended.

Card 20, The Resurrection

A million years ago the Doctrine of the Resurrection developed from the observation of the Cyclical Processes of Creation.

The Masters of Mu, sometimes called Lemuria, saw man as a part of nature, not apart from nature. That man is akin to nature not even the most rabid evolutionists will attempt to deny.

The Lemurian Masters realized that the link which binds man to all Nature is something far more than akinness. They saw in man something far greater than the flowers of the field.

Man is the crowning glory of all Creation. He is the god of all the earth,———a fact recognized even by the biblical makers (Gen.1:26), but not taught by the Mother Church.

For countless ages thruout the ancient world, the Crucifixion and Resurrection of a God was celebrated at the Vernal Equinox.

With the Resurrection of the Sun from the Winter Stolstice there came the Resurrection of the grass and flowers,,with dormant forests turning green with new foliage.

All Nature rose from the dead, said the Ancient Astrologers.

This cosmic event illustrates the Law of Cyclic Manifestation, the great law of the Universe which teaches us the inspiring lesson that Death is not what it seems to be.

For out of Death there cometh the Resurrection of the Immortal Entity. Paul

Card 20
Resurrection

said, "That which thou sowest is not quickened, except it die. . . .It is sown in
corruption; it is raised in incorruption. . . .It is sown a natural body; it is raised
a spiritual (astral) body. There is a natural body, and there is a spiritual (astral)
body. . . .As is the earthy, such are they also that are earthy; and as is the heavenly, such are they also that are heavenly. And as we have borne the image of the
earthy, we shall also bear the image of the heavenly" (1 Cor. 15th chapter).

It would be impossible to explain the matter more clearly. Kuhn said, "The
great Apostle (Paul) addressed himself ... to as lucid an exposition of the Spiritual
(Astral) Resurrection as is to be found anywhere in sacred literature. This 15th
chapter of I Corinthians marks the high point of spiritual (astral) sublimity reached
in the New Testament" (lost Light, p.573).

From the Death of Winter there comes in the Spring the Resurrection of all the
vegetation of the earth. Is man less than the flowers?

These facts of ages of observation taught the Ancient Masters that as the Law of
Cyclic Manifestation rules the vegetable kingdom, it must also rule the animal and
the humanal kingdoms. For the Law is one, and Life is one, and there could not be one
law for the Life of the vegetable kingdom and a different law of Life for the animal
and the humanal kingdoms.

If the flowers die and return to a Future Life, so does Man said the Ancient
Masters. The manifestation of Creative Life is cyclic in all kingdoms, and applies
to animal and humanal life as well and as fully as to vegetal Life.

Dr. James Clark wrote: "There is no Birth without Death, and no Death without
a Resurrection. All action in the Universe is dependent for its continuity upon
Cyclic Change; and as surely as Day follows Night, so must Life follow Death."--
Eternal Time.

Upon this solid foundation the Ancient Masters built their Doctrine of the Future
Life; and Paul said, "Behold, I show you a mystery: We shall not sleep (in death),
but we shall all be changed, in a moment, in the twinkling of an eye, at the last
trump; for the Trumpet (of Gabriel) shall sound, and the dead shall be raised incorruptible, and we shall be changed" (1 Cor.15:51,52).

In this interpretation of Card 20, The Resurrection, Ouspensky wrote:

"And I saw an icy plain. A chain of snow-covered mountains shut off the horizon. A cloud rose and grew until it covered a quarter of the sky. In the midst of
the cloud there appeared two fiery wings. And, behold, I saw (the Angel Gabriel) the
messenger of the Empress.

"I saw him raise his trumpet, and he blew a loud blast. And the plain trembled,
and the mountains answered with loud reverberating echoes.

"And one after another of the graves in the plain began to open, and out of them
there came forth people--young children and old men and women. And they stretched
out their arms to (the Angel Gabriel) the messenger of the Empress, and tried to
catch the sound of the trumpet.

"In that sound of the trumpet, I felt the warm smile of the Empress. And in the
opening graves I saw unfolding flowers and smelt their fragrance.

-70-

Card 20
Resurrection

"And now I understood the mystery of Birth and Death."--New Model of the Universe

The Seven Thunders

There is still another feature presented in Tarot Card 20 that is related to chapter 10 of the last book of the Bible, where it is said:

"And I saw another mighty angel (Gabriel) come down from heaven, clothed with a cloud; and a rainbow (Zodiakos) was upon his head ... and (he) cried with a loud voice as when he had cried, Seven Thunders uttered their voices.

"And when the Seven Thunders had uttered their voices, I was about to write; and I heard a voice from heaven saying unto me, Seal up those (mysterious) things which the Seven Thunders uttered, and write them not(as they are knowledge only for the Initiate).

"And the angel which I saw ... lifted up his hand to heaven, and sware ... that there should be Time no longer: But in the days of the voice of the Seventh Angel (Seventh Incarnation), when he shall begin to sound, the mystery of (the) God (Astral Man) should be finished (in his Seventh Incarnation), as he hath declared to his servants the prophets."

In the picture of Tarot 20, there are Seven lines radiating from the bell of the trumpet blown by Gabriel, signifying the Seven Incarnations of Man upon the earth, and this represented the Seventh, which finished the earthly career of Astral Man, for whom "there should be Time no longer," upon the terrestrial plane.

The correct interpretation of the symbolism of Tarot Cards 3 and 20 shows where the Church Fathers got their symbology and allegory contained in the New Testament.

These crafty biblical makers not only had possession of the 22 missing Trumps Major of the Ancient Tarot, but understood the interpretation thereof, and interpolated some of that interpretation in various parts of their New Testament, and wove it around their Jesus.

They state that their Jesus cried out with a loud voice (the voice of the Seven Thunders), (and) yielded up the ghost, ... "and the graves were opened (as pictured in Tarot Card 20), and many bodies of the saints which slept, arose" (Met.27:50,52).

That event in Man's existence called Death, which marks the transition from the terrestrial to the celestial world, was not regarded in ancient days as it now is in the Christian world.

There is no such state for anything as death, extinction, annihilation. There is no ending and no beginning. It is an axiom of science that something cannot come from nothing. And the something which comes must, under the universal law that Like begets Like, present in character, if not in degree, the qualities of the Creative Power.

And so, as Life in the terrestrial world comes from pre-existent Life in the

-71-

Card 20
Ressurrection

celestial world, that Life which comes has no beginning and no ending. In his "Pre-Existence Of Man" Prof. Hotema said:

"As the Macrocosm produces the Microcosm, under the law that Like begets Like, the Microcosm must illustrate and describe with perfect precision, the charecteristiss, qualities and properties of the Macrocosm."

Material forms change. They are created and disintegrated, but the uncreated Entities which inhabit the created forms never change.

CHAPTER XIII

UNKNOWN JOY OF DEATH.

Until the 15th century the Christian World had no hypothesis of creation except the account contained in the Bible, and it meant death by burning for an "enemy of

God" to question that account.

According to that theory, a God formed man of the dust of the ground, and breathed into his nostrils the breath of life; and man.

BECAME A LIVING SOUL (Gen.2:7).

That absurd, stupid, unscientific assertion never appeared in the Ancient Scriptures. It is purely a priestly invention,--a crude concoction of scheming men, and was designed to deceive the masses.

The Ancient Masters postulated a Law of Creation, and the soundness of their postulation has weathered the test of time. That Law was symbolized in their Magic

Wand, the Staff of Hermes, or Mercury, the Messenger of the Gods, and it is the subject of Card No. 1 of the ancient Tarot, titled The Magician, concerning which Prof-Hotema wrote:

"This symbol is to indicate the macrocosmic character of the Magician. It signifies that he embodies the Creative Principle (of the Universe), and personifies the tetradic qualities of Life known as Consciousness, Mind, Intelligence and Vitality." --Land of Light, p.51.

The basic principle of the ancient Law of Creation was signified by the White and Black Serpents of the Magic Wand, the Caduceus, and indicated the Universal

Principle of Polarity, which the Masters called the Double Law of Creation.

The only reference in the Bible to that great Law, appears in the statement that God created "male and female" (Gen.1:27).

Sexuality is another name for Polarity, and Polarity is not the product of Creation. It is a property naturally inherent in all Cosmic Elements, without which there would

be and could be no creation.

Religion is not founded on law. It is a cunning system of mind-conditioning invented by scheming men, and its purpose is to control the masses and reduce them to

a state of mental slavery. It is propagated in mental darkness and its success indicates a very law grade of individual consciousness.

The worst enemies of Religion are intelligent men. They are never religionists in good faith, but some often employ Religion as a means to gain some desired end, as a politician who is running for public office.

The Bible states that man "became a living soul" after he received from "God" the "breath of life." Before this "God" breathed into his nostrils the breath of life, man was only a lifeless form of "dust." Then the clever biblical makers preserved the harmony of their fairy tale by making Paul say, "the first man is of the earth, earthy; the second man is the Lord of heaven" (1 Cor.15:47).

We have shown that Paul knew there are Two Bodies In One. But he understood Anthropology and Biology too well to have made some of the ridiculous statements the crooked biblical makers attributed to him.

If the "soul" had a beginning as indicated in the Bible, then it does not possess the property of Immortality. For all objects and bodies that have beginnings, must have endings, as we have shown.

The scheming Religionists sought to salvage this defect by providing an exception to Universal Law. That's a good one. Upon that exception rests the very foundation of Christianity. Remove that exception and Christianity must collapse like a house of cards.

This exception to the great Law which has no exceptions, makes it possible for man to transform his temporal "soul" into an eternal "soul" by the simple process of putting his Faith in the Church Jesus. Nothing could be easier, and nothing could be more erroneous. Yet it fools the millions who want to be fooled.

According to the Ancient Wise Men, "Life and Death are but words, and both (conditions) are but the surface aspects of the deeper Being" (Bhagavad-Gita, chap. 2).

In the Ancient Philosophy, the words "die" and "death" did not imply extinction, The terms were employed to indicate re-birth, renovation, regeneration, resurrection.

In their study of natural phenomena, these Masters discovered no extinction of Life, such as we regard the words "die" and "death" to mean. Instead, they said, that which thou sowest is not quickened (in re-birth) except it die (1 Cor.15:2,36).

And so, what appears as "death" is really a New Birth. The Masters explained this by citing the "dying process" in the case of planted grain.

Planted grain does not "die". What occurs is a process of disintegration of the

-74-

Unknown Joy of Death

body of the grain, which reduces that created body to its original elements, while at the same time the Life of the grain, the Uncreated Entity, continues to live in the New Plant that springs from that created body of grain.

Nothing has died; there is no death. Death is the dream of a dunce, of a religionist, a scientist, a biologist, a chemist, an evolutionist.

We are taught by the Ancient Masters to regard Death as a process of change, of transition to a state wherein man's Cosmic Consciousness rules supreme, as it is then released from the limitations of the created body. Man is then able to recognize both aspects of his dual nature, and to sense the Astral Entity as his Real Self.

Transition, or physical death, is the change of physical Consciousness to Cosmic Consciousness, in which state "there is nothing covered, that shall not be revealed; and nothing hid, that shall not be known" (Mat.10:26).

We can cast more light on this strange point by citing the reports of those who have been on the brink of transition, but did not quite "pass over" (Ps.104:9). These reports all agree without a single exception.

We have reports in the case of a woman, believed for twenty-four hours to be dead; of a philosopher who was thought to be dead; of a truck-driver whose truck was demolished by a train and he lay unconscious for six days; of an engineer whose train was wrecked and who was unconscious for ten days; of a little girl who was believed for days to be dead.

The little girl was just old enough to talk well, and she described in a childish way what she experienced in her unconscious state. She had never heard the things she related, and yet her report was identical with all the others. And what did they report?

The secret of what occurs in man's mind at the moment of transition and subsequently, was taught to the Neophyte in the Egyptian Mysteries. The rites of these ancient dramas, "commencing in gloom and sorrow and ending in light and joy, dimly foreshadowed the peculiar passage of man from temporal mortality to celestial immortality."

Traces of this knowledge appear in the Bible in these words: "I will ransom them from the power of the grave" (Hos.13:14). Death is swallowed up in victory. O

Unknown Joy of Death

Death, where is thy sting? O Grave, where is thy victory?"—1 Cor.15:54,55.

A certain man lay on his death bed. He was a man who was noted for the trusting faith in his mind. He was a free-thinker, and many were the times when he had sat for hours discussing with friends the great question:

What is Death? What follows Death? Is Death the end of man?

Now, in his dying state, he was only minutes away from the true answer. Suddenly, his eyes opened wide as with a surge of new vitality. Then seemed to penetrate the very ceiling as though it were not there. Then a peaceful smile spread over his face. As the last breath was leaving his body, he whispered: "Ah! At last the Great Secret."

What was the Great Secret which he witnessed as he slipped out of his body? We shall relate that story as it was told by those who have been on the border-line of transition, but did not pass over:

First, there is a sense of surprising levity of the body. Before the unconscious person is willing to let nurse or doctor know that strange things are happening to him, he begins to sense that he is not lying so heavily.

He first thinks that it is the imagination. Then he begins to sense a pleasant warmth, and to feel that he could rise up in the air and nothing could atop him.

The room that was only a few feet distant, begins to appear to be farther away. This is due to the fading of physical sight, but he can still recognize those present.

Then he begins to sense a world devoid of space and time. This is the secret of the Fourth Dimension, not known to many. He can see everything, way back to the time of his birth, as in a dream. None of the persons mentioned above, including the little girl, had ever heard of the Fourth Dimension except the philosopher.

Then the voices of those present begin to grow faint, until it seems as if they were at the very end of a long hall. This state indicates a fading out of physical impressions.

Eventually, the unconsciousness man could see nothing but his body on the bed. Not with his physical eyes, but with his Astral Sight. He seems to be several feet above his body, gazing down at it.

Between him and his body a dim haze appears. The philosopher described it as the aura. Another said it resembled the Silver Cord mentioned in the Bible and described by Prof. Hotema in The Flame Divine (Eccl.12:6). Still another said it was similar to the umbilical cord, but not so solid.

They all saw something that seemed to extend from them to their body. It was that Cosmic Beam of Astral Light which ends in the Ego, and a description of which the student will find in The Flame Divine by Hotema.

Then, in the case of those who fail to "pass over," there is a sensation of sorrow that they must return to the body. The thrill of Astral Existence fills them with an impelling urge to let the changing process continue, so they'll not have to return to the body.

All the accounts agree that there is present a Dual Power: One that attempts to hold the in the body, and the other that tries to pull them away from the body. In that perplexing state, some of them waver.

Here is evidence of the Double Law of Creation of the Ancient Masters, unrecognized by modern science so far as Life and Man are concerned.

The Dual Power is the Positive and Negative Phases of Polarity. The Positive is electric and pulls. The Negative is magnetica and attracts.

If the Life Link, called the Silver Cord in the Bible, "breaks" at this moment, the Positive Phase succeeds and the body dies. If the Silver Cord holds fast, remains intact, the Negative Phase succeeds and the body lives.

The determining factor is the body's condition. If it remains suitable for the return of the Ego, the Silver Cord holds fast. But if the body's condition is not suitable for the return of the Ego, the Silver Cord "breaks" and the body dies.

The reader will find a fuller description of the Silver Cord in Prof. Hotema's work titled The Flame Divine.

When those who go thru this strange experience and return to the body, it is due to the magnetic phase of Polarity, and they feel a sensation of being cramped and closed in a narrow compartment. This indicated the return of their physical sensation

They begin to feel uncomfortable warm instead of the pleasant cooling sensation. They feel heavy and weighted down, as if there were a weight on their chest. It is hard to breathe; their eyelids are hard to open, but they slowly do,--and that is the first indication of their return to physical sonsciousness.

It may be several days some times before they are able to talk. But they realize all that is occurring around them.

This is the border-line state. The accounts not only all agree, but they relate the same understandable events. Such are some of the secrets of the Future Life known to the Masters and taught to the Initiates.

Harold Sherman wrote: "In time to come, when Death has been scientifically proved to be the Gateway to Another Life, all fear of Death will have been removed from the Consciousness of Mankind" (You Live After Death).

That time will not come until the last stone of the last church falls on the head of the last priest.

The Ancient Wise Men taught that the real Joy of Existence is experienced by the God of the Earth when he passes thru the natural Gateway of Death to the Glorious Future Life in the Celestial World of Eternity.

That no doubt is what the Bible means when it says, "Better is the Day of thy Death then the Day of thy Birth" (Eccl.1.7:1). The Bible adds:—

For there "is (the glory of) the Resurrection of the Dead.....The Dead shall be raised incorruptible.......For this corruptible (body) must put on incorruption, and this mortal (body) must put on immortality. (And then) Death is swallowed up in victory" (1 Cor. 15:42,52,53).

"And the gates of it (Celestial World) shall not be shut at all by day; for there shall be no night there (in the Bright Land of Eternality). (And) there should be Time no longer. And there shall be no more death" (Rev. 10:6;4,25).

And here it is, right in the Bible, according to which it is definitely clear that the Future Life rises in and from the Glorious Resurrection. That was the Secret Doctrine of the Ancient Masters which they concealed in their famous fable of the Crucified God and his Resurrection. And see what the Church did with it.

All leading nations of the Ancient World had that same fable; and we have it too. But now it has been changed by the Church so that it applies only to its Jesus.

Under the reign of Universal Law there is no Birth without Death, and no Death without Resurrection. All action in the entire Universe is definitely dependent for its continuity upon Cyclic Change; and as surely as Day follows Night, SO MUST LIFE FOLLOW DEATH.

The Bible confirms this; it says, "Behold, I show you a mystery: We shall not sleep (in death), but we shall all be changed (by Death to Immortality); in a moment, in the twinkling of an eye, at the last trump.

For the trumpet (of Gabriel) shall sound, and (we) the dead shall be raised incorruptible, and we shall be changed (by Death from Mortality to Immortality) (1 Cor.15:51,52).

Unknown Joy of Death

It should fill with exceedingly great Joy the mind of every person to know, that when he sheds his mortal body in the regular cosmic process called Death, it is for the express purpose of preparing him to "pass over" to the Future Life of Immortality, as the Bible clearly states.

These are the hidden facts of Creation which were taught by the Ancient Masters, who were not interested in swindling the masses nor in money-making schemes, but in discovering and elucidating the mysteries of Man and Creation.

The facts show that the Ancient Masters were scientific Anthropologists and Biologists of the highest order. They erected Temples not for the purpose of worshipping an imaginary God up in the sky, but in which to teach Man the nature of his constitution and the mystery of his Life.

We have followed the Bible as our guide and authority, and shown by its testimony that Man is constituted of a dual nature, of two bodies, one of which is called God Spirit in the Bible, and, according to the Bible, this God Spirit dwells in the earthy Temple, the Body of Man (1 Cor.3:16).

Where do we find Man in this duality? If he is not the corruptible, earthy Temple, then he must be the Uncreated Entity which dwells in that Temple. And if that be the case, then he is the God Spirit.

The God Spirit, the Real Man, unknown to us because we refuse to recognize him, clads himself in a Material Robe in the mother's womb, to make himself correspond with the physical world into which he will appear in the process called Birth, as we have stated in the discussion of Two Bodies In One.

We are confused because we refuse to recognize the facts, or because we insist upon creating a mythical God and putting him in man's place, thus pushing man back into a dark corner where he is not noticed.

When we dispense with this useless God, we begin to see the light. Then we grasp the fact that Man is the Ego who builds his own body, and is Mind, Consciousness, Intelligence and Vitality appearing in that body. We rise out of the fog as we formulate the Law of Creation which governs these phenomena.

But the sordid, corrupt institutions which rule our civilization, would soon

Unknown Joy of Death

perish and vanish if the deceived multitude knew the facts of Life and Death which are presented in this work.

The schools, colleges and medical institutions in which children and adults are educated and trained, have practically no other purpose than to mold and condition the Mind, so that the masses will meekly travel the beaten path which has been prepared by these organizations. And the day that some thinker gets out of step with the mob, he had better be silent, or he'll be liquidated and disposed of as an example to teach the others what to expect if they fail to follow the path of darkness.

Religious systems produce nothing but superstition, ignorance and darkness. They are the oldest, biggest and richest racket on earth, and they survive because they keep their dupes in darkness as to the actual nature of Life and the real meaning of

Theologists must always be vague in their statements as to the nature of Life, Death and the Future Life. They describe a place called Heaven above, and a place called Hell below, which are the abodes after Death of the Souls of men, the "good ones" going to Heaven above, a region of eternal bliss, and the "bad ones" going to Hell below, a region of perpetual punishment and torment.

As Christianity is based exclusively upon a belief in the Resurrection and the Hereafter, it should speak out more definitely and authoritatively about "life and death." But instead, we are asked to accept on Faith alone the doctrine of survival after Death. No kind of proof is presented.

Science can give us no help. It has almost nothing but ignorance in this field to offer us. It overtly admits that it knows not what Life is, hence it knows not what Death is. The great "scientists" declare that they know not what Life is. Two of these are Dr. Robert A. Millikan and Dr. Alexis Carrel. The former said:

"I cannot explain why I am alive rather than dead. Physiologists can tell me much about the mechanical and chemical processes of my body, but they cannot say why I am alive" (Collier's, Oct.24, 1925).

Carrel did not even attempt to describe or to identify Life in his writings that have come to our attention. He said:

"Our knowledge of the human body is, in truth, most rudimentary. It is impossible, for the present, to grasp its constitution. We must, then, be content with the scientific observation of our organic and mental activities, and, without any other guide, march forward into the unknown" (Man the Unknown, p.105).

When we began our study of Anthropology and Biology sixty years ago, the first shocking surprise we received was our discovery that science could give us no definite explanation of the nature of Life. We were told that science has explored Life down to a single cell of living matter, but exactly what makes that cell alive, is not known.

Why are Life and Death such unsolvable? Is it because there are no answers? no solutions? With so many other secrets of the Universe being solved and explained year after year, why do Life and Death continue to remain in the category of the mysterious and unknown?

This is not an accident. Nor is it because the mystery of Life and Death is unsolvable. There is a mighty good reason for this ignorance. A scientific solution of the mystery of Life and Death would utterly ruin Religion, the oldest, biggest and richest racket on earth.

The Christian world has no science of Anthropology and Biology, and never will have so long as Religion can prevent it. For it was Religion that destroyed that science in the 4th,5th, and 6th centuries A.D., and replaced it with a diabolical system of gross superstition and idolatry which ruled all Europe for more than a thousand dark years.

During that terrible nightmare of intellectual darkness, extending roughly from the year 500 to 1600 A.D., all factual knowledge of Creation was lost and destroyed, and was replaced with the fairy tales that appear in the Bible. Life and Death then became the most profound mysteries, and that state has continued until this hour.

Death was especially shrouded in the deepest of darkness, and pictured by Religionists as the most horrific catastrophe imaginable. For in Death the "soul"

mentioned in the second chapter of Genesis, was condemned to eternal damnation, un-

less the Church Jesus was accepted and worshipped as the only begotten Son of one of

the several Gods mentioned in the Bible.

Contrary to this false teaching of the Religionists, the Ancient Masters had

declared that the Day of Death is better than the Day of Birth, and clearly explained

the reason why to the Neophyte in the ceremony of initiation in the Ancient Mysteries,
those great schools which were crushed by the Christian Emperors of Rome.

One of the chief objectives of initiation was to teach the "man of darkness"

that his return to his original Glory in the Celestial World was thru the Gateway of
Death, that being the cosmic process of shedding the Corruptible and donning the Incorruptible.

When Man is born in the flesh, he comes into the visible world clad in a garment

which matches his material environment. That garment, his created body, he puts aside

as useless when he is Born Again out of the flesh in the cosmic process called Death,

and "passes over" to his Glorious Home in the Celestial World.

Man is actually a Son of the Sun, and, in spite of the illusion of appearances

and false teaching, he remains eternally the same and changes not, even while dwell-

ing on the earth in a form of flesh.

When we look at man, we see only his external appearance, and not his Real Self,

of which Prof. Hotema gives us a remarkable description in his work titled The Flame
Divine.

The Religionists had to destroy the literature of the "heathenish pagans", and

then cultivate and magnify the Fear of Death to drive into the Church the "dupes of

darkness," where they are assured by the crooked Clergy that their only hope of ever

escaping from the terrible torment following Death, is to believe that the Church

Jesus was the only begotten Son of a mysterious and unknown God way off up in the
sky, and that such a belief would win for them "everlasting life" (John 3:16).

Then there came those great men who refused to swallow these glaring falsehoods,

and they gave up their lives in the fires of the Mother Church that the masses might

Unknown Joys of Death

have some of the facts of Creation.

One of these glorious martyrs was Giordano Bruno, who was burned to ashes by the Church in Rome in 1600 for his "crime" of being "an enemy of God" because of teaching publicly the facts of Creation. He said;

"That which was seed at first, becomes grass, hence the ear, then bread, nutritive juice, blood, animal seed, embryo, man, corpse, then again earth, stone, or other material, etc.

"Herein we (observe the process of Creation and) recognize that which changes into all things and yet essentially remains ever the same. Nothing appears to be really durable, eternal, and worthy of the name of a principle, save Matter only.

"Matter as the Absolute includes within itself all forms and dimensions. But the infinity of forms in which Matter appears is not accepted by Matter from another, nor, as it were, only in external appearance. But Matter brings them forth from herself and bears them from her own womb.

"When we say there is Death, there is only the (change of) passing forward to New Life, a loosing of the old union which is the binding into a new" (Prof. Ludwig Buchner, M.D., in Force & Matter, 1884, p.20).

Such teachings enlightened the masses and marked the revival of the Sacred Wisdom of the Ancients, lost to the Christian world for a thousand years, and recovered by men who refused to swallow the falsehoods taught by the Church, and who sacrificed their lives in their grand work for the sake of suffering humanity.

The eternal ebb and flow of electrified particles, changeless in themselves, has been termed by scientists the transmutation of Matter; and science has cited countless cases thereof.

It is sufficient to notice the changes and cycles thru which universal Matter moves, and which science has partly followed with balance and measuring-rod, millionfold and ten millionfold, that they are endless and limitless. We clearly observe that creation and destruction, dissolution and resurrection, clasp hands everywhere in an endless circle.

Heraklitus said, "The Universe is made neither of gods nor of men, but has ever been and ever will be an Eternal Living Fire." And that Fire is the Universal Absolute in action, and may be called God, or Astral Light, or Asterial Electricity,

-83-

Unknown Joy of Death

or Cosmic Radiation, or what not.

Here we discover the God, the Fire, the Electrified Substance which appears to
us, in its condensed formation, as Matter. In harmony with this fact, the Bible terms
its God "a Consuming Fire" (Heb.12:29, etc.).

Then there appears the great Law of Polarity, the Universal Creative Agencies,
in the form of Fire and Freeze, Heat and Cold, Expansion and Contraction, Vaporization
and Condensation.

Heat reduces everything known to electrified gases, and cold condenses the gases
into every formation called Matter, of which are constituted every rock and plant,
every animal and man, every god and goddess, every object and organism of every kind
and description. At this point the student should study Cosmic Creation, 2nd ed. by
Prof. Hotema.

We may move the beginning as far back as we wish, and it is logical to assume
that Life always existed somewhere, sometime before it ever appeared in a created
body. There must first have been available some substance of which to create a body.
Then Life, acting in the capacity of Creator, began its creative work, and into existence came the bodies. And if Life has been able at any time to exist anywhere without a created body, why should we presume, as science does, that the Death of the body
is the end of Life?

The Ancient Masters declared that Man passes on to the Glorious Realm of the
Future Life thru the Gateway of Death. There is no other way. To imprison the Ego
forever in a mummified body, such would be the terrible solution of that magical
paradox concerning pretended immortalism in the same body and on the same earth. This
is the reason why the Masters asserted that the Day of Death is better than the Day
of Birth.

And now it will be enlightening to the religionists, scientists and biologists
to inform them, that what they habitually regard as L I F E is that activity which
results from motion.

The word Life is a descriptive term that applies to the action of created bodies.

Unknown Joy of Death

The term itself does not identify the Universal Animative Element that is responsible for the creation of the bodies and their activity.

There is no Life per se. Life has no essential existence of itself, says Prof. Hotema in his Cosmic Creation. Life is only a name applied to movements and changes occurring in Matter. These are the result of a peculiar Force residing in the Environment, said Herbert Spencer, the great Evolutionist of the 19th century. He called Life "A mode of motion."

Like all of the religioniete, scientists and evolutionists, Spencer was wandering in the wilderness. Life is not a Force inherent in the Environment. Life is an effect, a property of the Eternal Living Fire mentioned by Heraklitus.

Eliphas Levi said: "When after all the phantoms, thou shalt behold the shining of that incorporeal Fire, that sacred Fire with dancing radiance flashing formless thru the depths of the whole world, then harken to the Voice of Fire" (His. of Magic, p.67).

We shall proceed to show the reason why Spencer believed that Life is a force residing in the Environment. This secret is revealed by Dr. David J. Calicchio, M. D., in his book titled Electronology, copyright 1953, in which he asserts:

"Everything in existence (in the entire Universe) consists of (the Living Fire called) Electricity, which is manifest in different (primary) forms, concentrated as particles of Matter called electrons and protons, and electricity in rapid motion in the form of radiation.

"The entire Universe is (formed of and) moved by the positive and negative forces of electricity.....All the motions, visible and invisible, that transpire in the Universe, are produced by electricity, which is the universal agent" (and the Eternal Living Fire).

Science says that electricity is electrons in motion. An instrument has been invented which photographs the electron. The electron had to go thru nine feet of solid lead before its terrific speed was reduced enough to where a photograph of it could be taken.

Unknown Joy of Death

The elements of an atom are held together by tremendous electric voltage. When the formation of the atom is disrupted, these voltages are released in the form of terrific power. In the atomic bomb, the atoms of uranium or a similar substance, were broken in two--liberating the astounding force of two hundred million electronic volts per atom.

The Pythagoreans regarded Fire as constituting the Heart of the Universe, extending from the earth to the utmost limits of the Cosmos. They held that all things are derived from Fire, and strive ever to return to Fire.

The Sacred Fire of the Ancient Masters symbolized The Flame Divine, the great philosophy of antiquity that now lies buried beneath the ruins of their temples of the Ancient World.

Prof. Hotema shows in his work The Flame Divine, that Fire as Electricity, or Electricity as Fire, forms and moves everything known, from Astral Bodies to Atomic Particles. He said:

"When we gaze in a mirrow, we see only the physical form (of man), little suspecting that we are actually looking at Eternal Solar Man (the mighty Living Fire in human form.)

In Fate Magazine of October-1953, the Unknown Joy Of Death was described by a woman who passed over to the Future Life while undergoing surgery. She was quickly revived and the Ego returned to body when the physician performing the operation discovered the body was dead, because breathing had ceased and there was no heart action.

The student should understand by now that the Ego in the body is the cause of the body's functions, and the functions cease when the Ego leaves the body.

The woman said, "At some time during the operation, I (Ego) left my body. I was flying, and I knew it was no dream. For I had died. I knew it and I welcomed it.

"It was far more wonderful and glorious than any dream. I was no longer confined in my body. I was (free and) lighter than thought. I had no weight, no substance at all. I knew I was no longer a (physical) person.

"I was just an essence, just a vital spark, equipped with thoughts, feelings and senses. (Note: All senses of the body are the senses of the Ego--Hotema). The feeling above all else was that of extraordinary happiness.

-86-

Unknown Joy of Death

"I could hear magnificent music, and it seemed that I was the center of it. As I was savoring this ecstasy in its entirety, a voice within me commanded: 'You must go back.'

"And then I felt as if I were being pushed downward. I cried, I implored, but again came the command: 'You must go back.'

"And down I came, faster and faster, until, with a crash, I felt myself pushed into what seemed to be a box of lead, which my Ego knew was my body.

"When I told this to the doctor (after being revived), he informed me that toward the end of the operation, I had no pulse, no heart beat, no breath. I was dead. He said that he quickly inserted his fingers thru the incision of my body, and was able to massage my heart, trying to start its action. He succeeded, and I was alive again."

The Common Error

The Silver Cord, mentioned in the Bible (Eccl.12:6), is the Astral Beam of the Celestial World which is attached to the Ego, linking the Terrestrial Body with the Celestial Body.

This Beam is capable of almost infinite extension, and, regardless of the distance which may separate the body and its Ego, as in dreams, the Ego always returns to the body unless something happens to disturb, distort, or disrupt the Beam.

When the Silver Cord is loosened and the Ego is thus released from the body, a time of the highest importance comes to the Ego, and it cannot be too strongly impressed upon the friends and relatives of a "dying man" that it is a crime against the departing Ego to give expressions of loud grief and lamentations. For the Ego is then engaged in a process of supreme importance, unknown to modern science but well-known to the Ancient Masters, and much of the value of the past life depends upon the attention the Ego can give to that matter at this moment.

It is also a crime against the "dying" person to administer stimulants, which have the effect of forcing the Ego back into the body with a jerk, thus giving the "dying" person a serious shock.

Unknown Joy of Death

It is a pleasure to pass out of the body, but torture to be pulled back into it, to endure more suffering. It is the body which suffers, but the Ego, while in the body, shares in the suffering.

Some who have passed out of the body and been pulled back into it, have informed investigators that they had, in this way, been kept dying for hours, and had prayed that their friends and relatives would stop their mistaken kindness and permit them to pass on peacefully to the Future Life.

And another important matter is that the dead body should not be cremated nor embalmed until at least three days after death, as the Ego should be given that much time to free itself entirely fro the body.

To cremate or embalm the body before that much time has elapsed, tends to disrupt the Ego's work in etching the panorama of the past existence. This may have much to do with a person's remembering his

previous incarnations.

Harry Schnur, in his interesting book entitled Mystic Rebels, said:

"There is no death. The energy of the World Soul (Ego) is indestructible. It merely changes for another (body) the shell in which it is encased.

"The basis of metempsychosis is the conception that by the mere fact of incarnation in a mortal body, the Divine Purity of the Ego becomes tainted and the harmony distorted.

"Death is merely a change of domicile. The Soul (Ego) survives, and to some Initiates at a high level (of mental development), it is even given to retain memories of their former existences.

"Death holds no terror for the Pythagorean; neither does it exert on him the morbid fascination, the hope of 'heavenly reward' intermingled with the dread of cruel punishment, with which it is invested by other creeds.

"Death is only an apparent destruction. It has no reality" (p.13).

The Bhagavad-Gita says "He who hath found the Peace Within, and who hath been so illumined that he findeth his joy and happiness within himself, and knowing that within him is the Kingdom of Heaven, verily, he gaineth and Peace of the Real Self, because he hath blended himself (physical consciousness) with the Real Self, (Cosmic Consciousness).

"They from whom hath been removed the illusion of duality and separation, see all Life as One, and emanating from One. The welfare of the All becomes the welfare of the One to them, and to such cometh the Peace of the One.

"This Peace which passeth all understanding, cometh to those who knoweth themselves for what they are, rather than for what they seemeth to the smoke-blinded eyes of the world. They being freed from the bondage of desire and sense-passion, mastereth their thoughts with their Wisdom, and their senses with their thoughts" (Chap. 5).

"The Wise Man findeth his chief delight in that which is far above anything that the Mind can obtain by means of the senses, and having found it, he resteth in its Reality" (Chap. 6).

We shall conclude this chapter by quoting again the remarkable statement of Paul:

"We look not at the things which are seen, but at the things which are not seen; for the things which are seen are temporal; but the things which are not seen are Eternal" (2 Cor.4:18).

CHAPTER XIV

The Future Life

Literature that has lasted the longest is that which has based upon a desire for or an expectation of the Future Life.

It is as natural to desire Life after physical death, to hope for it, to seek knowledge of it, as it is to desire food, air, light. It is an unfortunate man who does not hope for a Life to come. It is an abnormal one who does not desire it.

The scribe of the Book of Job devoted chapter 14 to the subject, from which we take the following excerptions::

"He (Man) cometh forth like a flower, and is cut down; he fleeth also as a shadow and continueth not.   .For there is hope of a tree, if it be cut down, that it will sprout again, and that the tender branch thereof will not cease. . . .But man dieth, and wasteth away: Yea, man giveth up the ghost, and where is he?

"As the waters fail from the sea, and the flood decayeth and drieth up; so Man lieth down, and riseth not; till the heavens be no more, they sahll not awake, nor be raised out of their sleep. . . .If a man die, shall he live again?"

The evidence shows that the scribe who made those statements was not a Master.

The terms he used and the thoughts he expressed disclose that he was a "man of darkness." He had not found the Light. This we shall see more plainly as we proceed.

The universal expectation of Life after death rises out of conditions that are distinctly not physical. If the human mind had to depend upon only physical facts and regular vision of the eyes for the development of faith in a Future Life, it had remained undeveloped. No man who has looked upon a dead body, could ever have conceived the thought of a Future Life if he depended for evidence upon sight alone.

The very ancient Egyptian Book Of The Dead dealt principally with two segments of the Creative Cycle, (a) confinement of the Ego in the dark body, and the (b) Resurrection of the Ego therefrom. The first chapter dealt with the Glorious Resurrection, and the title of that great antique script was

"The Coming Forth By Day."

The title indicated the emergency into Light of the Ego from its dungeon of darkness in the body. It dealt with the Resurrection of the Dead. For the Ancient Masters consistently taught in all their philosophy, as we have previously stated, that the Ego, while inhabiting the body, is as Dead as it can ever be.

The chief difficulty in translating the Book of The Dead into another language

-90-

Future Life

is due to the gross ignorance of the blind, misguided, orthodox translators as to the
reverse meaning of the term Death.

Birth was Death and Death was Birth in the philosophy of the Ancient Masters,
and was so signified in all their symbolism. As stated in another place, the Black

Star in which appears Man with feet up and head down, represented Birth, incarnation,
confinement or imprisonment of the Ego in the body. This was also symbolized in Card

No. 12 of their Tarot, which portrayed Man with his head down, hanging by one foot.

The Death of the body is the Glorious Resurrection of the Ego. That is the
esoteric meaning of the symbolism of the Blazing Star, with man standing erect on his

feet and his head directed upward toward the Celestial World, at the top of Jacob's
Ladder (Gen.28:12), as described by Prof. Hotema in "Pre-Existence of Man."

This was symbolized in Card No. 20 of the Tarot, titled The Resurrection, and
presented in the Bible as the Born Again doctrine (John 3:3,5,7). In the Egyptian
Book Of The Dead the Resurrection was the coming forth of the Ka from the dark body

to the glorious Light.

The fraudulent misrepresentation of the Glorious Resurrection by the Church has
been serious and fatal. The church took the grand symbols and allegories of the

Arcane Science and fed them as veritable history to the brain-washed, mind-conditioned
masses, and then slaughtered and burned the wise ones who questioned and doubted.

While the mentally-enslaved followers of the mythical Christ were obliterating
in frenzied furry all traces of the Ancient Philosophy, there lay securely buried

from their devastating hands the great Egyptian Wisdom, protected from their predatory
zeal because of their own inability to decipher the mysterious hieroglyphs, as well

as their stupid misjudgment of the real value of that "pagan rubbish" as the Church
sneeringly stigmatized it.

The amazing message found in that "pagan rubbish" flashed a brilliant light in
a world of Christian darkness when the discovery of a slab of stone by one of

Napoleon's soldiers in 1799 disclosed the meaning of the baffling inscriptions on the
Egyptian monuments.

In the "Land Of Light" by Prof. Hotema is pictured the great Rosetta Stone that
told the startling story that amazed the Christian world. It contained the Key which

the unprejudiced researchers needed to unlock the secret meaning of the strange
Symbolism of the Ancient Masters, some of which appear in the front of this publica-
tion, and none of which could be interpreted in harmony with the Ancient Philosophy

until this Stone was discovered.

Much biblical reference to the period of "three days" in the grave concerns these
things, and there is a direct statement of the Resurrection imagery in Hosea:—

Future Life

"Come, let us return unto the Lord; for he hath torn, and he will heal us; he hath smitten, and he will bind us up. After two days will he revive us; in the third day he will raise us up, and we shall live (forever) in his sight" (Hos. 6:1,2).

The essential fact of the Glorious Resurrection was the ancient conception of the Essence of Being, the self-generating, self-sustaining power, ever renewing itself in visible phenomena, and getting the sick man well in spite of the blundering, obstructing work of the doctors.

The crudest error of conventional realigionism is the prevalent notion of a static eternity of the Ego after its Resurrection from the human body. This is another one of these delusions with which the despoiling of esotericism has afflicted the deceived masses.

The Living Entity is immortal, and its existence is never static. Immortality is thru the repetition of the Life Cycle; and that is why the Creative Cycles, endlessly repeated before our eyes in natural phenomena, are set as the symbols of our own existence.

The imperishable, immortal Solar Spark, called God Spirit in the Bible, which builds a body, is born into the physical world, and leaves it again at death, was typed by the Ancient Masters as the Crucifixion and the Resurrection. In what better way could it have been symbolized?

Confinement in the body was Crucifixion. The body, with the arms extended and the feet together, is a symbol of the Cross on which we hang in earthy life for evil purposes; that is why we are "cursed." We use the body to satisfy our lusts for sensation, greed, hate, gluttony, jealousy, and what not.

Liberation from this sordid state by the process of Death was the Glorious Resurrection with the Ancient Masters, and the Real Self, released from its imprisonment in the body, could roam at pleasure thru limitless space and universal thought.

The festival of the Resurrection was an astrological event, used as a type of teaching Immortality as attested by the time set for it. The event was celebrated all over the ancient world in the Spring, when all Nature was resurrecting from the death of winter sleep.

The Vernal Resurrection of the "dead" vegetation of the earth, the grass and trees in the cold zone, could hardly be surpassed for illustrating the universal miracle of the Resurrection of the Dead.

The Ancient Masters had no doctrine of the resurrection of a dead body. That unnatural, unscientific dogma was invented by the mother Church. And it required the slaughter of millions of people to force that dogma upon the masses.

Release of the Immortal Ego from confinement in the corpse was the Glorious Resurrection. "For this cause came Man unto this hour. Father, glorify thy name" (John 12:27,28).

Future Life

"Father, the hour is come; glorify thy Son (Man), that thy Son also may glorify thee (Ego). . . .And this is Life Eternal, that they might know thee, the only true god (Ego). . . .And now, O Father, glorify thou me with thine own self with the glory which I (Man) had with thee before the world was" (created) (John 17:1,3,5).

These passages are correctly understood when the Glorious Resurrection is understood.

Prof. Hotema said in his Cosmic Creation, "The experience of millions of years has shown, that when the earth became the home of Man, it became the partner of a being that is not only the King of Life and the Climax of Creation upon the earth, but who is as eternal as the very elements of which the earth is composed, and who was before the earth was created.

Liberation of the Ego from the dark body by the process of Death, ends the earthly confinement of the God, whose freedom from the earthy prison is gained at last

This God, the Ego, the Real Self, is that Spark of Primordial Fire which had no beginning and which existed before and is older than the Sun itself. This was regarded as a fact by the Ancient Masters and so recorded in their scriptures.

The evidence appears in the Bible that the scribe of the John gospel knew of this. He had possession of the ancient scroll of Proverbs, wherein it was written:

"The Lord (Creative Principle) possessed me (the Ego) in the beginning of his way, before his works of old. I was set up (existed) from everlasting, ... or ever the earth was . . . .Before the mountains were settled, before the hills, was I (the Ego) brought forth. . . .When he (Creative Principle) prepared the heavens, I (the Ego) was there."--Prov.8:22,27.

Accordingly, the scribe put into the mouth of his Jesus the statement: "Before Abraham was, I am" (Jn.8:58). That same statement applies to all humanity, and not to just one man.

Could purblind Christian theology have correctly divined the cosmogenetic and anthropogenetic facts so plainly expressed in these passages, it need not have left its gullible followers to grope in darkness for futile centuries, worshipping a mythical Christ, the "only begotten Son," that they might inherit everlasting life, which they already had in their own right, and the evidence of that fact appearing in their Bible.

We are now able to understand the factual meaning of the biblical passages, "O Death, I will be thy plague; O Grave, I will be thy destruction" (Ho.13:14).

-93-

Future Life

"I (The Ego) am he that liveth and was dead (while in the body); and behold, I am a-
live for evermore" (Rev.1:18).

The breaking of the Dawn of Light and the bursting from winter's captivity of
the Life Force in verdant Nature, are the kindred operations of natural phenomena

which have eternally been presented as constant reminders to Man of that unimaginable
transformation itno a Being of Light which awaits him at the summit of the mount of
mundane existence.

Insensible now to the subtle power of ancient symbolical philosophy, deadened and
unreceptive, because of a thousand years of brain-washing and mind-conditioning, to
the moving efficacy of ordinary natural glories, modern man neither heeds nor exults
at the rising of the Sun, and only feebly twitters a note or two of fayish poetry up-

on the arrival of the singing birds and the bursting buds of spring.

This mind-conditioned man is too blind to note that natural phenomena recapitu-
lates without end the physical type of that transfiguration which he has experiences
in endless cycles, and which, on the grand scale, is destined to occur for each of us
at the climax of our earthy career.

Cosmic phenomena presents, in the Water Cycle System, a striking textual illustra-
tion of the whole Cyclic Life Process. From the various bodies of water the Sun

elevates into endless space great masses of moisture, and a lowering of the tempature
causes that invisible vapor to condense and fall upon the earth as rain. That pro-

cess depicts the Creative Cycle.

The Water Circuit bristles at every turn with analogies of the Life Circuit.
Every phase of the Water Cycle is visible except that one in which the water is loft-
ed, by solar force, into the sky as invisible vapor.

The whole Life Cycle is perceptible except the one arc in which the Ego returns
to its asterial home in the aeriferous world. But science stubbornly stands upon its
firm denial of the Ego's existence after the death of the body on the sheer ground

of its vanishment from sight.

Nature's typology indicates that, like the invisible vapor which rises to the
sky and returns as rain, so will the Ego rise and then return again to the earth,
clad in another body. The Ego must be existent in the interim, for something cannot
come from nothing.

As the Water Cycle is complete in spite of the one invisible segment, so is the
Life Cycle complete in spite of the one invisible segement, as Prof. Hotema so clearly and convincingly explained in his three works, (a) Pre-Existence Of Man, (b) The

Flame Divine, and (c) The Soul's Secret.

The cosmic process called Death is as natural as Birth. It is not understood,
neither is it taught in the schools that the Life Element moves in cycles as the
Water Element does.

Dr. James Clark in his remarkable book, "Eternal Time," makes this striking

Future Life

observation:

"The life and death phases (of Man) are coexisting essentials in continuing (Man
's) existence; and the existence of either (phase) without the presence of the other
(phase) is an impossibility.

"The realization (of the nature of the Creative Cycle) in full understanding
that no state (of existence) can ever begin unless some other previous state is end-

ing, enables us at last to see with clear vision that any man may spend a life-time
in action in a Life Form (body), studying in any of the many 'Temples,' and no matter
whether the lofty architecture, nor the awe-inspiring design of the High Altar as seen

in St. Peter's Rome, or the Cyclotron in Harwell, England, there is only one incident
of major and fundamental importance that can ever happen to Man.

"And this incident provides all the reason there can ever be for having lived--
which is the insuring of the Cycle of the Eternal Action of Life, and thus creating
with certainty the supreme privilege and reward of living again--HE CAN DIE! (For the
Future Life depends upon death--Hotema).

"There is no observable action in the entire Universe that is not fundamentally
dependent for its continuity upon Cyclic Change; and as surely as Day follows Night,

SO MUST LIFE AGAIN FOLLOW DEATH."

That philosophy is scientific, naturalistic, meets the test of universal law,
is hoary with age, and was taught by the Ancient Masters ten and twenty thousand years

ago. It appears in the Bhagavad Gita as follows:

"Know thou, O Prince of Pandu, that there was never a time when I, nor thou, nor
any of these princes of the earth, were not; nor shall there ever come a time hereafter when any of us shall cease to be.

(The Life Element had no beginning and has no ending--Hotema.)

"As the Ego, wearing this material form, experienceth the stages of infancy,
youth, manhood and old age, even so shall it, in due time, pass on to another body,
and in subsequent incarnations shall it again live(on the earthy plane), and move,
and play its part.

"Those (wise men) who have attained the Wisdom of the Inner Doctrine, know these
secrets, and fail to be moved by aught that cometh to pass in this world of change.
To such, Life and Death are but words (of description), and both(words) are but the
surface aspect of the deeper being."

According to universal law, the teachings of the Ancient Masters, and the findings of leading biologists, when Man goes thru the cosmic process called Death, he
simply changes to another state, as mentioned by Paul who said:

"Behold, I show you a mystery: We shall not sleep (in death), but we shall be

changed" (to Immortality) (1 Cor.15:51).

Future Life

The only "mystery" surrounding Birth and Death rises from ignorance and false teaching. And this "mystery" is necessary to support the biggest frauds on earth.

Dr. Clark said, "All the mystery surrounding Life is dependent upon the continuous creation (by the teachers) of the unknown."

Man fears Death because the Mother Church invented a terrible Monster as a judging, vengeful, terrifying Demon who will punish, and punish, and punish us for each error we have ever committed. This scheme was invented to drive the mind-conditioned masses into the Church and it has been a grand success.

Death is not an ending, an extermination, a finality. It is a creative process that releases the Ego from physical bondage so it may return to a place of peace and joy in the Astral World.

The gnostic poet Phocylides declared, "After we have left our earthly garments, we shall be gods, for an immortal and incorruptible Entity dwells in the body." And the word "god" appearing in the Ancient Scrolls invariably referred to Man.

The Ancient Mysteries demonstrated to the Neophyte in the ritual of initiation, the duality of every living thing, from a flower to a man, explaining that the physical body is only the vehicle of the immortal Asterial Entity.

A tomb inscription in Italy, dating from the fourth century B.C., states, "It is a beautiful mystery which comes to us from the gods, to the effect that Death for man is not an evil but a good."

Enthusiasm for Death was not only a funeral formula, but an infatuation which drove men to sucide. "Life is but deception and misery," declared Theognis. Sophcles said, "The first good thing to be born, and the second is to die as soon as possible."

Hegesias of Cyrene, surnamed Peisithanatos (he who persuades men to die), taught that Death was preferable to Life. His disciples killed themselves in such numbers that Ptolemy Philadelphus closed his school at Alexandria and prohibited him from teaching.

In accord with the law that governs all Elements and Entities, the Ancient Astrologers taught that the Ego is without beginning and without end. If it had a beginning, it must have an ending; for all things which begin must in time come to an end.

Nor is the Ego formed in the body as taught by theology. The Church Fathers never copied from Ancient Scrolls the statement that God formed man of the dust of the ground, and breathed into his nostrils the Breath of Life, and man BECAME a living soul (Gen.2:7).

The Church Fathers resorted to many schemes and tricks of fraud and deception in the compilation of their "Holy Bible", the "Inspired Word Of God."

CHAPTER XV

Reincarnation

"Both thou and I have passed thru many births......Mine are known unto me, but thou knowest not of thine."--Bhegevad-Gita, Chap.4.

"Tell me, O Aspirant, that the understanding may bring him back that knowledge which was his in former births".--Blavatsky, Voice of Silence.

"Ye which have followed me, in the regeneration (reincarnation) ...ye shall sit upon twelve thrones, judging the twelve tribes of Israel" (Mat. 19:28).

The memory of antecedent incarnations comes to a few. There seems to be no chance remembrance. It all follows a fixed law, and appears to come when the Higher Self finds that the personality is prepared--when the physical brain has been conditioned to vibrate to some extent in response to the will of the Higher Self.

That seldom occurs now, due to the deleterious effect of a thousand years of intensive brain-washing and mind-conditioning of the masses by the Mother Church. When it does occur, he who experiences the phenomenon must keep silent, or be considered irrational or imprisoned for insanity.

Another reason why we fail to recall our past lives, rises from the fact that in our evolution we have gone thru many embittering experiences which, if remembered, would so depress and discourage us, that we would make little progress. Hence, it is for our benefit that the mind cannot reach back and bring up these experiences into our memory.

Many think that if they could remember who they had been in the past, it would all be joy and pleasure; but in the great majority of cases it would be the reverse.

Men's Sense Powers are definitely astral forces working thru the physical organism. As astral Man becomes robed in a physical body, he usually loses much of his omnipotent, omnipresent, omniscient Astral Senses, and he also loses, except on rare occasions, conscious contact with the Astral World.

In another place we have said that when Astral Man creates a body and confines himself therein, he naturally suffers a serious diminution of Consciousness, and his memory of antecedent incarnations grows dim and generally vanishes completely, leaving in its place, in some cases, only a dim intuition of previous lives.

With the literature of the ancient Pagans destroyed to hide certain knowledge

Reincarnation

which the Mother Church wanted to conceal from the masses, we are forced

to fall back on the Bible for evidence as to the belief of ancient people in Reincarnation. And we are surprised to see the Church Fathers, perhaps unwittingly, let some of the data

on Reincarnation slip into the Bible.

When the gospel Jesus asked his disciples the question, "Whom do men say that I the Son of Man am?" they replied:

"Some say that thou art John the Baptist; some, Elias; and others, Jeremias, or one of the (ancient) prophets" (Mat.16:13,14).

According to this, Elias who had been dead seven hundred years, was reborn as John the Baptist, which furnishes more evidence to indicate the ancient people believed in Reincarnation.

Julian, the last Pagan Emperor of Rome, believed that he was the Reincarnation of Alexander the Great.

Some amazing instances have been reported of those who do appear to have retained enough Cosmic Consciousness to recall definite events that occurred in their lives

many centuries before. Colonel Roches, of France, used hypnotism to take his subjects back thru what seemed to be a series of antecedent incarnations.

Henry Blythe wrote a book on Reincarnation, published in 1956, titled The Three Lives Of Naomi Henri, in which appears this statement:

"Stimulated by the now-famous Bridey Murphy case (of Reincarnation), the London Daily Express commissioned the well-known British consultant hypnotist, Henry Blythe, to conduct a similar experiment for them.

"Mrs. Naomi Henry, thirty-two-year-old mother of four children, was selected as the subject, and sessions were arranged with witnesses and press photographers present. These sessions, which took Mrs. Henry on a journey into a pre-conscious world, were each preserved on tape recordings.

"Unlike Ruth Simmons, her American counterpart (in Bridey Murphy), Mrs. Henry startled one and all by revealing under hypnosis two previous identities, one as Clarice Hellier, an unmarried English nurse who lived around the turn of the century, and another as Mary Cohen, a rural Irish girl who married and lived to old age in the 19th century.

"Then the London Daily Express withdrew its support of the experiment, not because they were not convinced, but because it became awed and afraid.

"As Mary Cohen, Mrs. Henry was questioned as to her state of experience subsequent to the age and date she gave of her death. Mrs. Henry, lying on a couch, stopped

ed breathing. Her pulse was felt. Her heart was not beating. The skilful Blythe awakened her quickly, but the press decided it was playing with fire.

"Blythe then pursued the experiment independently, to establish still another identity. Of the Three Lives of Mrs. Henry, the authoritative journal, Prediction, significantly comments: 'Those people who are indifferent to Reincarnation, may

think again after reading this extremely interesting book.'"

An unusual 12-inch long-playing record, made from the actual Naomi Henry experiment in hypnosis as to Reincarnation, has been produced in England. It presents the

voice of Mrs. Henry as she described under hypnosis her life as Mary Cohen, the girl she was in 1790. This record has created a sensation in England.

One A. R. Martin claimed no psychic gift, but he was able to take the subject back thru antecedent incarnations. He made a study of hypnotism, and became interested in the work of Dr. Cannon, who could send the subject's memory back to the moment of birth, but no further.

In his book, "Researches into Reincarnation and Beyond," Martin recounts some fifty of his thousands of cases. Not every subject could be sent back thru his preceding incarnations. The ability to relax is vital.

A certain orthodox minister visited Martin, and was sent back thru several of his previous incarnations. Some of the experiences caused the minister to burst into

tears, and he asked whether it were conceivable that he had gone thru such experiences

Martin replied, "If all this were not in your mind, it could not be coming out."

The minister saw himself in the past as a ruler of a tenth century Chinese province. During this review he lectured on Buddhism, chanting in Chinese. Later,

he saw himself in a Swiss chalet as an old man, futilely trying to comfort a distraught daughter.

Perhaps more amazing was the fact, that in all these instances, his present physical body assumed, as if by magic, the posture, tone and bearing suitable to the

character that he was each time in previous incarnations.

Once he appeared to suffer such agony from thirst, that a doctor present could hardly be restrained from administering to the "dying" man. But when this "dying" man came out of the trance, he did not want any water.

Another reason why we do not more often remember antecedent lives on the terrestrial plane is, that at each incarnation the Solar Man clads himself in a new body, the brain cells of which have never responded to the past conditions, and only when the brain is capable of responding to the memory stored up in the Higher Self, can that memory be impressed upon the waking consciousness. In other words, the

personality, per se, cannot remember the past because it has experienced only the present life.

Still another reason is that many of our previous lives have been so common-place and trivial, that they have registered little of value in the Higher Self, hence have

Reincarnation

little of importance to remember.

When a student is earnestly and sincerely seeking for Light, and striving toward self-mastery, he frequently develops a strong impression that he has a special work

to do. In the case of a well-balanced mind, this is generally the first glimmering of of a bona fide memory of the past. It is often given in dreams, and perhaps is

remembered in the waking consciousness as an intangible impression.

The amazing story of Shanti Devi, whose claims as to a previous life reportedly were proven by investigations, has been related many times in the twenty-seven years

that have passed since it first created a sensation.

At the age of four, Shanti began telling her parents of her previous life. What impressed them was that she gave exact details of her previous incarnation.

Her husband's name, she said, was Chaubey. They had lived with their children in a house in Mathura, a small town some 75 miles wouth of New Delhi, until she had

died at the age of 32.

In 1936 a committee of fifteen prominent men investigated Shanti's claims. The girl, then 10 years old, was taken to Mathura, and without any hesitation she led them directly to her "husband's house," in which, to their marked surprised, there

did live a man named Chaubey.

This man, under questioning, verified numerous details which Shanti claimed to know as his "wife," including his favorite dishes, and the very spot in a bed-room where his wife, Lugdi, kept money hidden. His wife, he said, had died at a certain

hospital on October 4, 1925, when she was 32 years old.

Today, plump and bespectacled, Shanti leads an austere life in an ancient house in one of the oldest sections of New Delhi. A spinster, she occasionally visits her

former "husband's" house in Mathura.--Fate Magazine.

Five thousand years ago and more, the Ancient Masters discovered certain ways that made it possible to pierce the wall which blocks off the memory of antecedent lives, just as modern hypnotists are doing now. In this way they not only reveal

the surprising fact of Reincarnation, but also furnish proof of the Future Life.

The Ancient Masters realized that the revelation of Reincarnation and the Future Life were mysteries that should be kept a guarded secret, and disclosed only to the Initiates whose minds had been prepared in advance for this higher knowledge.

If the masses in general knew the facts, many people would have little desire or inclination to go on and endure the burdens and suffer the hardships of earthly

life, where despots oppress and tyrants rule, even under the best form of government which men have been able to devise.

Reincarnation

And so, it is well that Man is in darkness as to his Real Self while dwelling in the body on the earth plane, in order that he will go on and live out his allotted

time on the earth in the flesh. It is a wise provision of Cosmic Creation that closed the Human Mind at this point, so that it could not definitely envision the fact

of the Future Life and prevision the existence of the Bright World of Eternality.

It is also the deliberate work of the Mother Church that has caused much of the unrest and misery in which the masses live and labor. The Religionists are careful

to present a horrific picture of Life in the Flesh, and a much worse one of Death and Hereafter. And so Man, while he lives in the Flesh on the earth, dwells between two

fires, two dreaded conditions. me

The Church teaches Man to spend his days thanking an imaginary God for the "earthly blessings" he "enjoys," and to depend on the Church for the help that only

it can give him in making "peace" with that Tyrannical God of Vengeance, in order that his "Soul" may not suffer eternal torment after Death.

In a Book of Canon Law, approved by Pope Leo XIII, it is written: "The death sentence is a necessary and efficacious means for the Church to attain its ends."

Just what are "Its ends"? An excellent answer to that question is found in a History of the Inquisition. That is a book that every one should read.

It was published in 1926 by The Truth Seekers Co., 38 Park Row, New York 8, N. Y., 645 pages. Read it and shudder and shake as you think of what the people of Europe

went thru during the Dark Ages of one thousand years.

The only measure of protection that stands between the Man who refuses to live in the darkness of Religion and his death, is the Federal Constitution, which was

written by a group of Free Thinkers who knew the terrors of the Mother Church and sought to protect therefrom the people of this nation.

The Glorious Resurrection

CHAPTER XVI

The Universal Fable

The ancient drama, celebrating the Crucifixion and Resurrection of a God, symbolized the universal process of the Creative Cycle which the Ancient Masters recognized in this changing world of illusion to be in constant operation on all levels of cosmic activity.

This annual event was widely celebrated in the ancient world so far back in the night of time, that all traces of its origin are lost. The stone monuments which have resisted the ravages of time, reveal that it was celebrated thousands of years ago.

The farther back we go, the more evidence appears to prove that one form of religion was followed by all races, and this evidence is confirmed by what Ptolemy Philadelphus (309-246 B.C. discovered, when he offered rich rewards for all kinds of religious manuscripts and scrolls for his great library at Alexandria.

The wise men of all nations, impelled by a desire for the reward, journeyed to Alexandria with their choicest scriptures, By this means Ptolemy succeeded in securing some 280,000 of the most ancient and valuable scriptures in the world.

He had his chief librarian make a careful comparison of the various writings, and was amazed to find that all the ancient systems of worship were copies of one original system, one universal religion, which varied in different countries only as the customs of the people varied.

Marcus Aurelius said, "The Universe, compact of all things, is One. Thru all things there runs one Power," and that Power is Cosmic Electricity said Dr. David J. Calicchio, who wrote:

"It is now generally admitted that an electrical force is at work in the Universe, and Electricity has accordingly been divided by scientists into two district parts, (a) concentrated electricity in the form of electrons and protons, and (b) waves of electricity classed as radiation.....The entire Universe is moved by the positive and negative forces of electrical action. And all operations in nature, in the earth and in its elements, are carried on by this same power" (Electronology).

Chronological forgeries have been freely used to make one particular system of religion and its God older than all the rest. And traces of the universal religion have been preserved by inscriptions on stone monuments and temples of all races and nations, in spite of the destructive work of various religious fanatics, who strive to make their system appear as the only true religion.

The annual celebration of the ancient drama was timed to correspond with the Vernal Equinox, when the venerative rays of the glorious Sun caused the "resurrection" of the "dead" grass and flowers, and the "dead" forests to turn green with New Life in the spring.

Behold, said the Ancient Masters, that all nature "rises from the dead."

They regarded Man as the God of Creation, and his journey thru the dark, terrestrial world here below, ended at the rim of the eastern horizon at the Dawn of Easter Light. The ark shrine of the God reached at last the Bright Land across the Eridanus River, never trodden by the dark feet of Death, and the enthralled God disembarked to take a new journey in the majestic ship of the Celestial World, beginning its voyage across the shining sea of Eternity.

The cabin door was open wide for the God of Glory to enter, and he advanced amidst the joyful acclaim of his host of devotees, as they hailed him who had risen victorious over the dark world of imprisonment, and they shouted in a grand chorus, "Death is swallowed up in victory. O Death, where is thy sting? O Grave, where is thy victory? (1 Cor.15:54,55).

To limn the actuality of this marvelous experience lies beyond the limit of any language, and the Ancient Masters never attempted to describe it orally or literally. They resorted to symbols and fables and these they interpreted in their Temples to the Neophyte who proved by test to be worthy to receive the Sacred Wisdom.

The 15th chapter of Paul's Epistle to the Corinthians discloses that he attempted to do this, and that chapter marks the climax of creative sublimity attained in the New Testament. "Its oracular grandeur," wrote Dr. Kuhn, "should have lifted up the body of Christian tehology far above the mists of controversy that overhang it as to the question of the corporeal resurrection." He wisely added:

"But the later formulators of orthodox theology looked askance at Paul and classed him as a heretic. They would have ousted his Epistles from the canon if they had

dared. For he had grown in disfavor among them. His philosophy was not in accord with the policy of the literalizers of the religious (ancient) drama. He was the

exponent of the Orphic-Platonic Wisdom of the Chaldeans and Egyptians, which they had come to revile. He indited more than one of the grandest chapters in their Bible;

yet they frowned upon him because his writing was not in harmony with their cult-Christianity. His was Cosmic Christiantity. It was embodied in terms of Platonic

Gnosticism, the very flower of Greek rational mysticism. Orphic paganism glows thru-out the 15th chapter of Corinthians (in spite of the garbled and distorted manner in

which it appears in the Bible to put the Church Jesus into the picture). The sublimest chapter in the Christian Bible is purely pagan (ancient) philosophy" (Lost Light, p.573).

Dr. James Clark made what may be termed a highly important prophetic statement

when he said:

"The day may not be far distant when Man can depart from what now appears to

have been the greatest of all his follies in evil,—the indoctrination of our inno-

cent children in the multitude of superstitious beliefs, thru which the various

systems of social control and enslavement have been perpetuated and fastened upon

each succeeding generation" (Eternal Time).

Realizing how hard it is to kill money-making schemes, we cannot be so opti-

mistic as to believe that these systems to which he refers will come to an end with-

in the next thousand years.

Neither should we forget that Religion is the oldest, and the biggest and the richest racket in the world. It is based on the Great Fear of Death, and its foundstion is destroyed when the facts of Death are properly presented and well understood.

1960 Professor Hotema explores and explains symbolism and its relation to ancient science, the universal fable of our numerous crucified saviors; the mysterious resurrection of Christ and its true meaning. By understanding ancient terminology, we can correctly interpret the true meaning of the biblical stories, for Hotema understood that the New Testament was a parable and one must comprehend the ancient knowledge, in order to interpret the parable.

Chapter Headings: Symbolism; Ancient Science; Crucified Saviors; Great Mother of the Gods; Mysterious Resurrection; Birth of Gods; Light; Two Bodies in One; Ancient Terminology; Mystic Sleep; Life Cycle; Swindle of Mythography; Unknown Joy of Death; The Future Life; Reincarnation; The Universal Fable.